Foreword

I've now been preparing children for their 11+ for over 30 years and have also gone through the process with my two boys. I've found that children who are well prepared enjoy the real test day even though it is stressful. Practising test papers is an important part of that process as it teaches the hidden skills of concentrating for a long time, filling in the answer sheets correctly, dealing with the stress of questions they can't do or ones they have never seen before and most importantly, coping with the pressure of a timed exam. They will learn various exam strategies that they haven't been taught before such as always put in a guess with multiple choice questions if they don't know the answer and don't spend too long on a question you are struggling with when you might be able to answer two or three others in that time.

The tests should also be used as an indicator of topics which your child doesn't yet know or is less confident with. Focus on these topics before doing the next test. There are two sets of answer grids included in this book to allow you to redo a test at a later date if necessary. The answer grids and answers section can be cut out of the book for ease of use.

Do read my 'Notes to parents' section as it gives tips and hints on how to tackle these papers with your child for maximum advantage. If you find a particular section of the test poses a problem, look at the Gulliford Tutors set of 11+ books on Amazon.co.uk as I have written books for the topics I have found my students needed extra practice on.

Good luck and keep up the hard work!

Contents

	Page
Foreword	1
Notes to parents	3
Set A paper 1	7
Set A paper 2	27
Set B paper 1	47
set B paper 2	69
Answer grids Set A	89
Answer grids Set B	99
Duplicate Answer grids Set A	111
Duplicate Answer grids Set B	121
Answers	133
Record your child's score	143

Notes to parents

11+ tests in schools

Each school will have its own format for their test day. This will include different order of papers, different timings and different sections within those papers.

The test papers in this book attempt to give your child experience of a broad list of 11+ components. However, it is important to try a wide variety of published test papers so they learn to be flexible and roll with different types of questions and designs of answer grids. Many schools try to include new types of questions and sections in their papers each year so it is important to give your child the confidence to deal with something new and not panic.

How to use these papers

If these are the first papers your child has seen:

Talk through the examples in each section and let your child try to answer the questions UNTIMED. Help with those questions they can't do or get wrong. If you find weaknesses in knowledge, practise more of this type of question. Look at the full range of 11+ books by Gulliford Tutors including Shuffled Sentences; Synonyms & Antonyms missing letters; CLOZE; My 11+ Vocabulary book and 11+ Short Maths .

You will find two sets of answer grids at the back of the book. Start using these grids straight away as part of the practice paper experience as it is a skill in itself. You will find two sets of answer grids to each paper. Once you have gone through incorrect questions together and practised topics which were weak, it is often a good idea to ask your child to redo the paper later in the week and see if their score has improved – it gives them confidence.

If your child has completed test papers before:

Try to do the papers in exam conditions:
- Work in a quiet room.
- Give your child a pencil, rubber, question paper and answer grid.
- A calculator or dictionary must not be used.
- Time each section separately and accurately. Give a time warning halfway through (some schools also give a 2 minutes warning.)
- Have a clock in view at all times for your child. Most schools ban anything other than an analogue watch.
- Don't explain any terms or questions during the timed test – your child needs to gain the confidence and coping strategies to figure out what to do or move on without panicking – explain everything at the end of the paper.
- These days, many schools ask that all calculations are done on the question paper and they do not give out paper for calculations. Check with the school you are trying for and practise in that manner they use which might be that the children must not write on the question paper.
- The children MUST write their answers in the answer grid as it is only this which is checked.
- They must mark their answer neatly in the answer grid and must not put more than one answer unless the question asks for this.
- The clock does not stop for any reason so explain to your child that they must not leave the room once the test has started or ask to go to the toilet as there is not enough time and they could miss a whole section. Explain that there is time before the exam and in the break between papers to go to the toilet.
- If they make a mistake on the answer grid, they must rub it out properly and insert the correct answer.
- Once completed, mark the paper correctly and record scores of each section plus the overall score for the paper. This allows you to see where your child has weaknesses so that you can focus in on these before completing another set of papers.

If speed is an issue, talk about it and try out strategies which help your child speed up.

Always be positive whatever the score : be mindful that your child is only 9 or 10 and will want to do well. They get frustrated with themselves if it doesn't go to plan. A good strategy is to say that doing papers is about fixing any mistakes and spotting topics they haven't learned yet so you or their tutor can put that right.

Tips for success:

- make sure you don't ask your child to complete a test paper when they are tired or there is a lot of activity in the house – it always ends in disaster!
- Explain to your child that the exams have some really tricky questions in them to see which children panic and spend the next five minutes on that one question or which children circle the question, move on and come back at the end if they have time.
- Tell your child to try to answer every question but for multiple choice questions, always have an educated guess on ones they don't know.
- In our experience, when you start timing tests, scores drop dramatically. Don't panic! Usually scores increase by about 5% with each successive set of papers.
- Never do papers bit by bit over numerous days. Completing whole papers in one go encourages concentration and mental resilience.
- Organise at least two mock mornings at home in the run up to the real test. Again, your child needs the experience of concentrating and working quickly for two whole papers with only a 15 – 20 minute break in between.

If done well, the 11+ preparation experience can increase your child's self-confidence and self-esteem and give you both the chance to work as a team which really is an advantage when they need help in the run up to GCSE s! Obviously, the main objective in 11+ preparation is for success on the day but actually, often the most important outcome is that your child is confident on the day and enjoys the experience rather than being thrown into an unknown situation which they find distressing. If they come out smiling and say it was OK, then you've done a good job!

Set A Paper 1

11+ CEM (Durham) Style Practice Paper

Gulliford Tutors

Copyright c Gulliford Tutors 2021
All rights reserved. No part of this book may be reproduced or transmitted in any form or by any means without written permission of the author.

Test 1A

Instructions

1. You can use the question book to write on when working out answers.
2. Write your answers in the seperate answer booklet provided. Mark your answer by drawing a line in the correct numbered box.

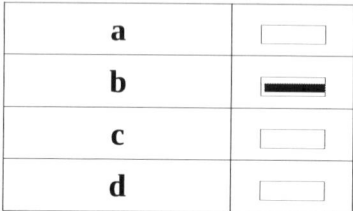

3. If you need to write a number in the answer book, mark the digits in separate boxes.
4. Write in pencil only.
5. If you need to change your answer, make sure that you rub out the incorrect answer completely before writing in the new answer.
6. Answer as many questions as possible. If you have time left at the end of a section, go back and attempt any questions in that section which you left out before.
6. Do not move onto the next section until instructed to do so.
7. You will have 45 minutes to complete the whole paper, however each section has a time limit. You will be told the time limit at the start of each section.

Section 1 : Comprehension

Instructions on how to answer this section:

Read the passage of writing given to you then answer the questions writing the letter A,B,C or D corresponding to the correct answer on your answer sheet. Go back to the passage as many times as needed to find the answer.

Example:

Comets

Comets are small celestial bodies which orbit the Sun. They are mainly icy blocks made from frozen ammonia, methane and water and only contain a small amount of rock. Due to this, they are often nick-named 'dirty snowballs'.

Comets are made up of four components: the nucleus, Coma, dust trail and ion trail. The nucleus is made up of rocky material and can have a diameter of anything between 10 km and 100km. The Coma is the cloud of gases which are vaporised as the nucleus is heated as it approaches the sun. These gases are usually a mixture of water vapour, ammonia, carbon dioxide. The trails are tiny dust particles blown away as the nucleus heats and ionised gases are blown away from the Sun.

1. What is the Coma of a comet?
a.   Rocky material and dust
b.   A cloud of gases
c.   A mixture of oxygen and carbon dioxide
d.   A trail of ions

The correct answer is b a cloud of gases. Therefore you would put a line through the b box on Q1.

Section 1 : Comprehension

> There are 15 questions in 12 minutes

What to do: read this passage carefully and then answer the questions.

The Last Lesson by Alphonse Daudet

I started for school very late that morning and was in great dread of a scolding, especially because Monsieur Hamel had said that he would question us on grammar, and I did not know the first word about it. For a moment I thought of running away and spending the day out of doors. It was so warm, so bright! The birds were chirping at the edge of the woods; and in the open field back of the sawmill the Prussian soldiers were drilling. It was all much more tempting than the rules of grammar, but I had the strength to resist, and hurried off to school.

When I passed the town hall there was a crowd in front of the bulletin-board. For the last two years all our bad news had come from there—the lost battles, the draft, the orders of the commanding officer—and I thought to myself, without stopping, "What can be the matter now?"

Usually, when school began, there was a great bustle, which could be heard out in the street, the opening and closing of desks, lessons repeated in unison, very loud, with our hands over our ears to understand better, and the teacher's great ruler rapping on the table. But now it was all so still! I had counted on the commotion to get to my desk without being seen; but, of course, that day everything had to be as quiet as Sunday morning. Through the window I saw my classmates, already in their places, and Monsieur Hamel walking up and down with his terrible iron ruler under his arm. I had to open the door and go in before everybody. You can imagine how I blushed and how frightened I was.

But nothing happened. He saw me and said very kindly, "Go to your place quickly, little Franz. We were beginning without you."

I jumped over the bench and sat down at my desk. The whole school seemed so strange and solemn. But the thing that surprised me most was to see, on the back benches that were always empty, the village people sitting quietly like ourselves; old Hauser, with his three-cornered hat, the former mayor, the former postmaster, and several others besides. Everybody looked sad; and Hauser had brought an old primer, thumbed at the edges, and he held it open on his knees with his great spectacles lying across the pages.

While I was wondering about it all, M. Hamel mounted his chair, and, in the same grave and gentle tone which he had used to me, said:

"My children, this is the last lesson I shall give you. The order has come from Berlin to teach only German in the schools of Alsace and Lorraine. The new master comes to-morrow. This is your last French lesson. I want you to be very attentive."

My last French lesson! Why, I hardly knew how to write! I should never learn any more! I must stop there, then! Oh, how sorry I was for not learning my lessons, for seeking birds' eggs, or going sliding on the Saar! My books, that had seemed such a nuisance a while ago, were old friends now that I couldn't give up. And M. Hamel, too; the idea that he was going away, that I should never see him again, made me forget all about his ruler and how cranky he was.

Then, from one thing to another, M. Hamel went on to talk of the French language, saying that it was the most beautiful language in the world—the clearest, the most logical; that we must guard it among us and never forget it, because when a people are enslaved, as long as they hold fast to their language it is as if they had the key to their prison. Then he opened a grammar and read us our lesson. I was amazed to see how well I understood it. All he said seemed so easy, so easy! I think, too, that I had never listened so carefully, and that he had never explained everything with so much patience. It seemed almost as if the poor man wanted to give us all he knew before going away, and to put it all into our heads at one stroke.

"My friends," said he, "I—I—" But something choked him. He could not go on.

Then he turned to the blackboard, took a piece of chalk, and, bearing on with all his might, he wrote as large as he could:

"Vive La France!"

Then he stopped and leaned his head against the wall, and, without a word, he made a gesture to us with his hand: "School is dismissed—you may go."

1. Which country is this set in?

a. Holland

b. England

c. France

d. Spain

2. What does ' a great dread of a scolding' mean?

a. He's worried he'll burn his hand on the school gate

b. He doesn't like school

c. He's anxious that he will be told off

d. He's fearful of going to school

3. What are the Prussian soldiers doing?

a. Digging for oil in the fields

b. Practising their marching skills

c. The dentist is checking their teeth

d. Setting up camp in the fields

4. What is the beginning of the school day usually like?

a. Noisy and chaotic

b. Quiet and disciplined

c. Still and silent

d. Hurried and repetitious

5. What does the words ' in unison' mean?

a. One at a time

b. Continuously

c. In the same room

d. All together

6. What had the narrator hoped would distract the teacher so he wouldn't be spotted arriving late?

a. The noise and chaos

b. The interesting lesson

c. People being in the wrong desks

d. The teacher facing the blackboard

7. Why is the teacher's ruler described as 'terrible' ?

a. Most rulers are made of wood

b. It is used as a form of punishment

c. It is ugly and loud when used

d. It doesn't draw a straight line

8. What was so surprising about today's class?

a. Monsieur Hamel called him 'Little Franz'

b. The teacher was beginning without him

c. The empty benches were filled with villagers

d. The narrator was frightened

9. Why was M. Hamel leaving?

a. M. Hamel was going off to fight

b. M. Hamel only spoke French

c. Schools were offering more languages now

d. Only German was to be taught

10. Why had the order come from Berlin?

a. It was World War II and they needed spies

b. Germany had invaded and controlled everything

c. Berlin is the capital of France

d. Berlin was the nearest big city

11. M. Hamel is described as 'cranky'. What does this mean?

a. His joints are stiff

b. He expects silence in class

c. He tells great stories

d. He's bad tempered

12. Why does M. Hamel use the words 'enslaved' and 'prison' ?

a. He is going to be arrested by the German soldiers

b. Many locals have been put in prisons

c. The Germans have taken away their freedom

d. The Germans have sold them into slavery

13. What part of speech is the phrase 'they had the key to their prison' ?

a. Metaphor

b. Simile

c. Idiom

d. Alliteration

14. Why does the narrator suddenly understand the grammar lesson today?

a. It was an easy lesson because the villagers were there

b. The teacher was explaining it slowly

c. The teacher was quickly explaining everything in grammar

d. He was finally paying attention

15. Why did M. Hamel write 'Vive La France!' in big letters on the board?

a. He was being patriotic

b. He hoped France wouldn't die

c. It means Goodbye

d. He loved teaching French

End of this section – Stop here .

Section 2 : Synonyms

Instructions on how to answer this section:

A synonym is a word with the same meaning or nearly the same meaning as another word.

E.G. **Large**   a. small   b. enormous   c. full   d. complete

The answer is b. enormous because it has the same meaning as large.

Section 2 : Synonyms

| There are 20 questions in 9 minutes |

What to do: Find the synonym for each given word . Remember to mark the corresponding letter on your answer sheet.

1. **rigid**	a. flexible	b. stiff	c. glum	d. revolve
2. **brutal**	a. bully	b. impolite	c. vicious	d. Imbecile
3. **united**	a. joined	b. football	c. applaud	d. agree
4. **aware**	a. clothed	b. concentrate	c. empty	d. alert
5. **capable**	a. useless	b. succeed	c. compete	d. competent
6. **harmless**	a. innocuous	b. dangerous	c. devious	d. constant
7. **ample**	a. scarcity	b. plenty	c. excessive	d. empty

8. argument	a. fable	b. conversation	c. concord	d. dispute
9. innocent	a. guilty	b. blameless	c. trivial	d. roll
10. unimportant	a. insignificant	b. doubtful	c. tiny	d. incorrect
11. certain	a. dubious	b. appropriate	c. accurate	d. definite
12. forgiveness	a. kind	b. clemency	c. hopeful	d. futile
13. random	a. unusual	b. organised	c. haphazard	d. indifferent
14. unblemished	a. flawless	b. unified	c. scarred	d. inaccurate
15. prosperous	a. arrogant	b. successful	c. capable	d. outspoken
16. durable	a. feeble	b. safe	c. hard	d. sturdy
17. conclusion	a. end	b. decide	c. answering	d. subdued
18. unsurpassed	a. overtaken	b. unbeaten	c. unnoticed	d. average
19. coax	a. thoughtful	b. argue	c. temptation	d. persuade
20. perplexed	a. inexplicable	b. unchanging	c. confused	d. enticing

End of this section – Stop here.

Section 3 : CLOZE - Wordbank

Instructions on how to answer this section:

A CLOZE test is a passage of writing with words left out. These words are found in a list of words above the passage called a wordbank. Link the word letter to the question number and mark the letter on your answer sheet.

a. Cold	b. waves
c. blue	d. summer

The 1._____ day was hot and the 2. _____ shimmering sea was enticing. However, when I jumped in, the water was   3. _____ - and the 4. _____ too high.

The 1._____summer_____day was hot and the 2. _____blue_____ shimmering sea was enticing. However, when I jumped in, the water was   3. _____cold____ and the 4. _____waves_____too high.

1) d   2) c   3) a   4) b

Section 3 : CLOZE – Wordbank

There are 12 questions in 6 minutes

What to do: Read the passage below and fill in the spaces with the appropriate word from the wordbank. Put the letter for that word on your answer sheet. Complete the wordbanks within the time given.

Aesop's Fables - The Lion and the Bull

a. account	b. cauldrons	c. departed	d. downfall
e. offence	f. thanks	g. approaching	h. company
i. desiring	j. evidence	k. preparation	l. slain

A Lion, greatly 1. _____ to capture a Bull, and yet afraid to attack him on 2. _____ of his great size, resorted to a trick to ensure his 3. _____. He approached the Bull and said, "I have 4. _____ a fine sheep, my friend; and if you will come home and share him with me, I shall be delighted to have your 5. _____." The Lion said this in the hope that, as the Bull was in the act of reclining to eat, he might attack him and make a meal of him. The Bull, on 6. _____ the Lion's den, saw the huge spits and giant 7. _____, and no sign whatever of the sheep, and, without saying a word, quietly 8. _____. The Lion inquired why he went off so abruptly without a word of 9. _____ to his host, who had not given him any cause for 10. _____. "I have reasons enough," said the Bull. "I see no 11. _____ whatsoever of your having slaughtered a sheep, while I do see very plainly every 12. _____ for your dining on a bull."

End of this section – Stop here.

Section 4 : Shuffled Sentences

Instructions on how to answer this section:

Each question is a sentence which has been shuffled around. However there is also an extra word which is not meant to be there. Unshuffle the sentence to find the word which does not fit in the sentence. Link the word letter to the question number and mark the letter on your answer sheet.

For example:

The purred happily barked cat

The sentence is: The cat purred happily

so the word not used is 'barked'.

Section 4 : Shuffled Sentences

There are 12 questions in 6 minutes

What to do: Unshuffle the sentence to find the word which does not fit in the sentence. Link the word letter to the question number and mark the letter on your answer sheet.

1. jumps lead dog a the on walks she
    a. lead   b. walks   c. jumps   d. the

2. starry a day cold night it and was
    a. day   b. night   c. it   d. starry

3. angry swarmed hutch hive bees the around the
    a. the   b. hutch   c. angry   d. hive

21

4. the ripped when it was batter parcel arrived
   a. ripped   b. it   c. batter   d. arrived

5. to our party will be me my family coming entire
   a. our   b. my   c. entire   d. me

6. to refuse meat eat vegetarians sugar
   a. sugar   b. meat   c. vegetarians   d. to

7. dad into table leg the bumped arm
   a. leg   b. table   c. into   d. arm

8. shoes the rubbing pinched small her
   a. rubbing   b. her   c. small   d. the

9. green the and lush dry was garden
   a. dry   b. lush   c. green   d. the

10. with be angrily mum knew upset would our us we
    a. upset   b. us   c. angrily   d. would

11. off bow of the jumped the boys bough tree the
    a. off   b. bough   c. bow   d. of

12. under star tree the excited their put children presents the
    a. presents   b. star   c. excited   d. their

End of this section – Stop here .

Section 5 : Numerical Reasoning

Instructions on how to answer this section:

In this mathematical section, you need to read the question and calculate the correct answer.

You will then need to write your answer in your answer grid. Firstly, write the answer in the space at the top of the grid, then you MUST write the individual digits in the column grid below, making sure that you mark each digit in the correct column grid for that specific question number.

What is 15% of 140?

The answer is 21.

Therefore write 21 in the space at the top of the grid and the digits 2 and 1 in the column grid as shown below.

2	1
0	0
1	1 ▬
2 ▬	2
3	3
4	4
5	5
6	6
7	7
8	8
9	9

23

Section 5 : Numerical Reasoning

There are 21 questions in 12 minutes

What to do: read the questions carefully and then calculate the correct answer.

You will then need to write your answer in your answer grid. Firstly, write the answer in the space at the top of the grid, then you MUST write the individual digits in the column grid below, making sure that you mark each digit in the correct column grid for that specific question number.

① What is 20% of 140 ?

② What is $\frac{8}{9}$ of 72 ?

③ James has £20. He spends £6.41. How much change will he get ?

④ What is 18% of 400 ?

⑤ Calculate 15^2

⑥ Find angle x

(triangle with a right angle, 36° angle, and x° angle)

⑦ $4c - 2 = 22$ Solve this equation to find c .

⑧ $5 \times 7 + 12 \div 3 =$

⑨ B = 50 – 2(3n+1)   Find B when n = 3

⑩ 45 × 145 + 55 × 145 =

⑪ A shelf holds 26 books. How many books will 8 shelves hold ?

⑫ What is the midpoint between 18 and 32 ?

⑬ Write $\frac{19}{25}$ as a percentage.

⑭ If 6 rulers cost £2.52, how much would 10 rulers cost ?

⑮ How many metres in 0.088 km?

⑯ The ratio of boys to girls in a class is 2 : 3 . If there are 10 boys, how many girls are there?

⑰ A train journey departs at 08:39 and arrives at its destination at 09:27. How many minutes is the journey ?

⑱ There are 6 black, 3 golden and 3 white puppies in a litter. 4 of the black and 1 of the golden puppies are sold. The owner decides to keep one of the remaining puppies. What is the probability it is golden ?

⑲ 21 cm^2 The area of a rectangle is 21cm^2. The length of the rectangle is 4cm longer than the width. How long is the length?

⑳ £3.99 x 5 =

㉑ A minibus holds 14 children. 60 children are going on a school trip. How many minibuses will be needed?

End of this section – Stop here .

End of this test paper.

Set A Paper 2

11+ CEM (Durham) Style Practice Paper

Gulliford Tutors

Copyright © Gulliford Tutors 2021
All rights reserved. No part of this book may be reproduced or transmitted in any form or by any means without written permission of the author.

Set A paper 2

Instructions

1. You can use the question book to write on when working out answers.
2. Write your answers in the separate answer booklet provided. Mark your answer by drawing a line in the correct numbered box.

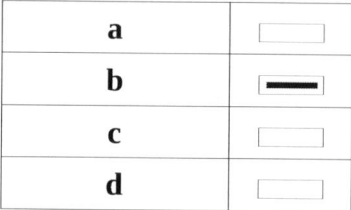

3. If you need to write a number in the answer book, mark the digits in separate boxes.
4. Write in pencil only.
5. If you need to change your answer, make sure that you rub out the incorrect answer completely before writing in the new answer.
6. Answer as many questions as possible. If you have time left at the end of a section, go back and attempt any questions in that section which you left out before.
6. Do not move onto the next section until instructed to do so.
7. You will have 50 minutes to complete the whole paper, however each section has a time limit. You will be told the time limit at the start of each section.

Section 1 : Numerical Reasoning

Instructions on how to answer this section: In this mathematical section, you need to read the question and calculate the correct answer.

You will then need to write your answer in your answer grid. Firstly, write the answer in the space at the top of the grid, then you MUST write the individual digits in the column grid below, making sure that you mark each digit in the correct column grid for that specific question number.

What is 15% of 140?

The answer is 21.

Therefore write 21 in the space at the top of the grid and the digits 2 and 1 in the column grid as shown below.

2	1
0	0
1	1 ▬
2 ▬	2
3	3
4	4
5	5
6	6
7	7
8	8
9	9

Section 1 : Numerical Reasoning

What to do: read the questions carefully and then calculate the correct answer.

You will then need to write your answer in your answer grid. Firstly, write the answer in the space at the top of the grid, then you MUST write the individual digits in the column grid below, making sure that you mark each digit in the correct column grid for that specific question number.

There are 40 questions in 35 minutes

①   What is the value of the 8 in 687650?

②   Which is the smallest number:

        0.24   2.41   24.1   0.18   0.2

③   Mary and Megan each have a parcel. Mary's parcel weighs 2¼ kg. Megan's parcel weighs 1.8 kg. How many more grams does Mary's parcel weigh than Megan's?

④   A bag of dog food weighs 1.5 kg. Jane gives her dog 60 grams per meal and feeds her twice a day. How long will the bag of dog food last?

⑤   C is the midpoint of the line A to B. What are the coordinates of C?

        (___ , ___)

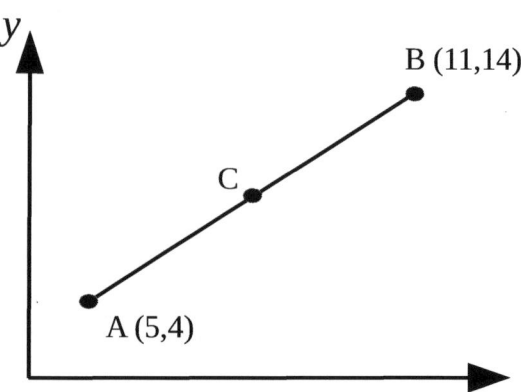

⑥ An advertisement in the local paper costs 15p per word plus a standard charge of £2.50.

   a) What is the cost for an advertisement consisting of 9 words?

   b) How many words would be in an advertisement for which the charge is £4.30?

⑦ 4 cups of tea and cake cost £3.70. The cake costs 90p. What is the cost of a cup of tea?

⑧ The duration of telephone calls made from an office was recorded and plotted in a bar chart.

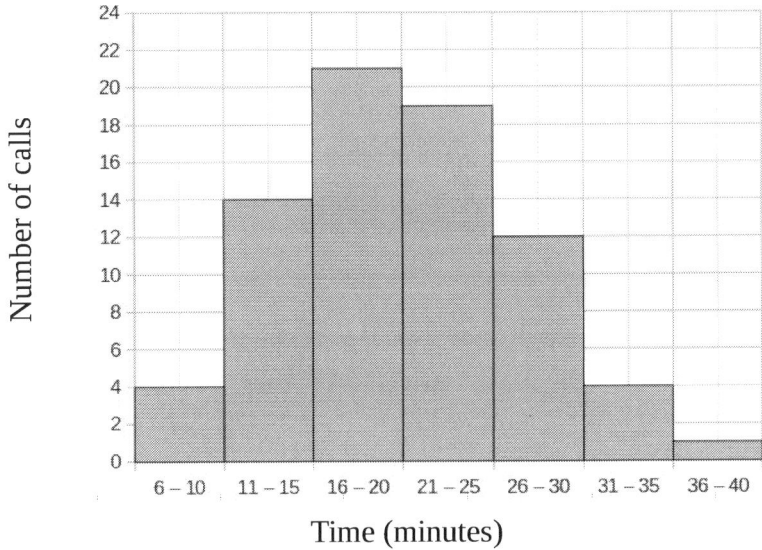

   a) How many calls were made in total?

   b) What was the modal duration in minutes?

   c) How many calls were over 25 minutes?

⑨ On January 1st the temperature was -5°C at 6 am. It increased steadily by 3°C every hour. What temperature was it at 10 am?

⑩ Through how many degrees does the minute hand turn through in $2\frac{1}{4}$ hours?

⑪ Jane lives with her dogs. In total, Jane and her dogs have 26 legs. How many dogs does she have?

⑫

Train Timetable			
Station	Train 1	Train 2	Train 3
Exmouth	14:32	14:52	15:32
Lympstone	14:41	15:01	15:41
Topsham	15:03	15:23	16:03

a) How long does it take Train 1 to get from Lympstone to Topsham?

b) Mary has to be in Topsham by 3:30pm. It takes her 25 minutes to walk from her house to the station in Exmouth. What is the latest she can leave her house?

c) Peter catches the 15:32 train from Exmouth to Lympstone. He stays in Lympstone for 3hrs 20 minutes. He catches the train back to Exmouth. Assuming he doesn't have to wait for a train, what time will he catch the train back to Exmouth?

⑬ What is the probability of picking a vowel in the words "Eleven Plus"?

⑭ Jane has 6 numbers on cards. She has lost one of the cards. The remaining cards have numbers 7, 4, 5, 10, 3. If the original set of 6 cards had a mean of 6, what is the missing number?

⑮ A garden is a rectangular shape with a flowerbed surrounded by a grass lawn.

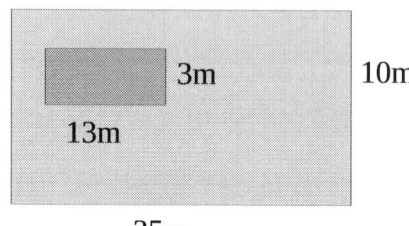

a) What is the area of the lawn?

b) It costs £10.99 for a pack of grass seed. Each pack covers 15m^2. What will it cost to have enough seed to cover the lawn?

⑯ Patricia is completing a running challenge. She runs 1km per day the first week; 2km per day in the second week; 3km per day in the third week etc. How far will she have run in total after 5 weeks?

17) A book store logged their book sales on one day. The results were put in this table.

	Paperback	Not paperback	Total
Fiction	96	32	
Non-fiction	8		28
Total			

a) How many books were not paperback?

b) How many paperback fiction books were there?

c) How many non-fiction books were there?

d) How many books did they sell altogether?

18) Fred cycles 8 miles to work each day at an average speed of 16 miles per hour. If he gets to work at 08:50, what time did he leave home?

19) Paula has a lot of wooden cubes with each side of length 5cm. She makes a larger cube with them with each side 30cm. How many of the small cubes does she use?

20)

Glasgow				
41	Edinburgh			
70	72	Dundee		
149	126	54	Aberdeen	
168	164	138	102	Inverness

In this table, the distances between these cities is in miles. Use it to answer the following questions:

a) How far is it from Edinburgh to Dundee?

b) What is the furthest city from Edinburgh?

c) Jane travels from Glasgow to Aberdeen, stopping off at Dundee on the way. Then she returns home direct from Aberdeen to Glasgow. How far has she driven?

㉑ Brian makes concrete using sand and cement. He can mix the two in two ways:

         Mix A   **Mix B**

    Sand and cement   Sand and cement

    in the ratio 3 : 1   in the ratio 1 : 2

If he mixes 24 litres of each mixture, how much sand will be used in total?

㉒ The area of the right-angled triangle on the right is equal to the area of the rectangle on the left. Work out the value of x.

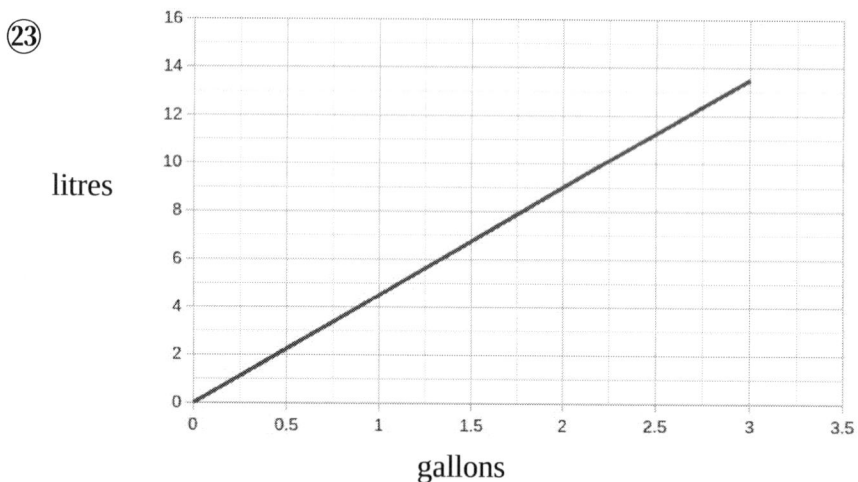

20 cm   12 cm   30 cm

㉓

litres vs gallons conversion graph

Using the conversion graph above, answer the following questions:

a) Convert 2 gallons into litres.

b) Jane's car uses 1.6 gallons on her journey. Mark's car uses 10 litres. Which person uses more fuel?

c) A lorry holds 400 gallons of oil. How many litres is this?

24) A pattern of dots is:

  a) How many dots would there be in the 7th pattern?
  b) What is the nth term formula for this sequence of dots?

  a. 2n - 4   b. 4n – 4   c. 4n – 2   d. 2n + 6

25) There are 240 different plants in a garden. 30% of these are roses. The roses are either red, white or yellow in the ratio 5 : 2 : 1. How many flowers are white roses?

26) A painter charges a call-out fee of £50 and then £15 an hour. On a particular job he charges £125. How many hours did he work?

End of this section – Stop here .

Section 2 : Non-verbal Reasoning

Instructions on how to answer this section: Look at each of the examples of how to solve these non-verbal reasoning questions. Each method is different so you must look at each example carefully.

Example 1 for Q1-5

Changing patterns: Look at the example given on the left. Work out how the left-hand shape has changed to the right-hand shape. Now on the right-hand side of the line, work out how the given shape would change in the same way.

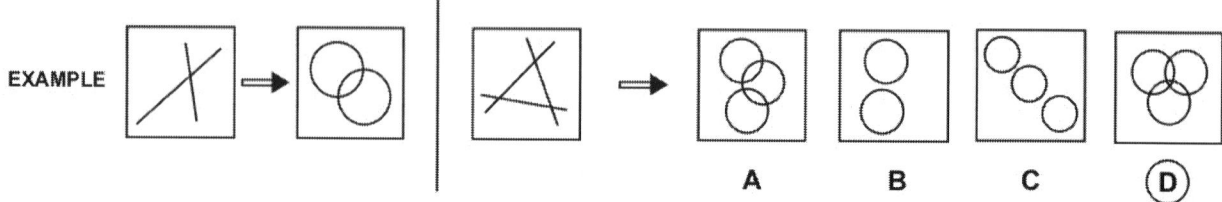

D is correct because the number of lines equals the number of circles and number of times the lines cross equals the number of intersections of the circles.

Example 2 for Q6-15

Cube nets: Look at the example given on the left. Work out which of the cubes is made from the cube net on the left.

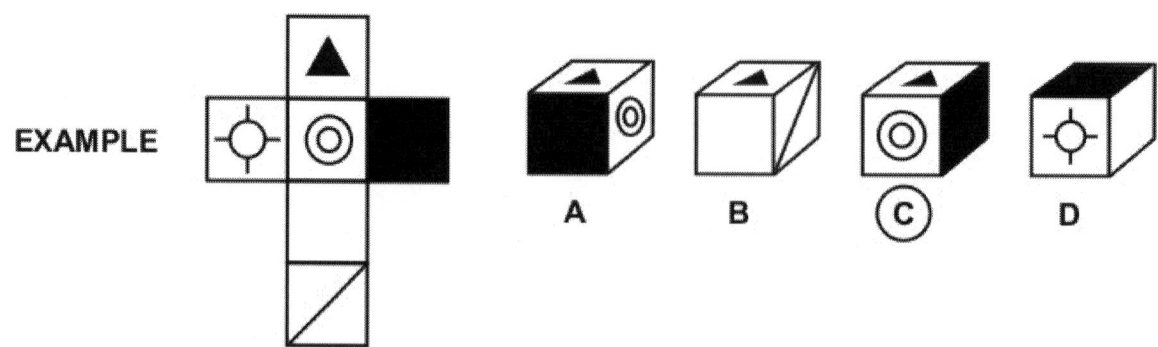

C is correct because on the net the triangle is directly above the double circle and the black is directly to the right of the double circle.

Example 3 for Q16-20

Complete the series: Look at the series of pictures and work out what is happening. One of the series is missing. Work out which picture fits in the blank space in the series.

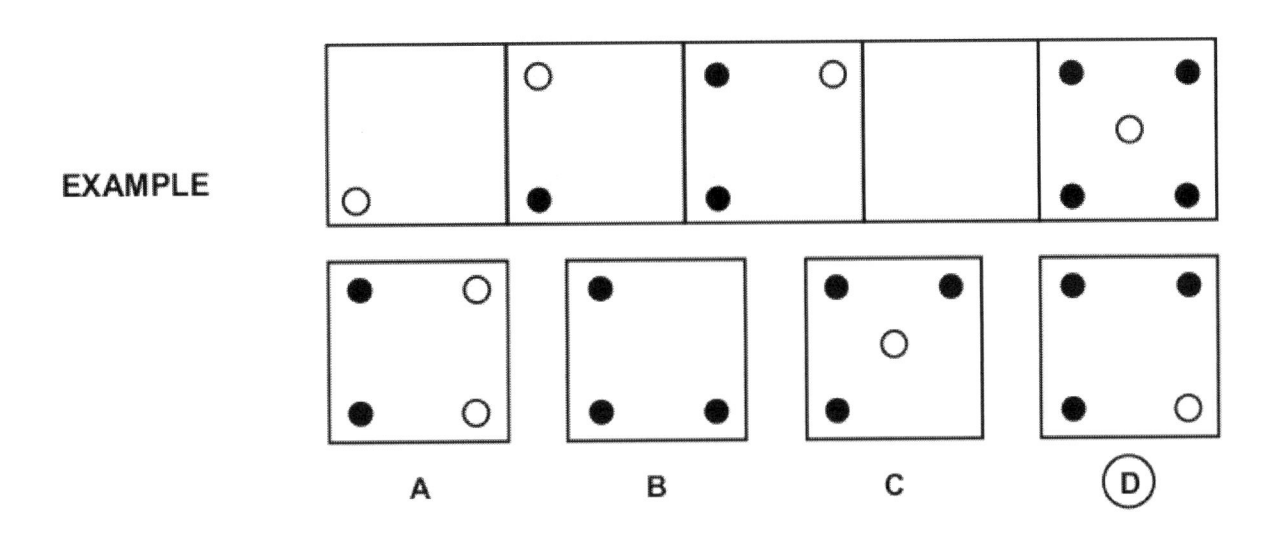

EXAMPLE

D is correct because each square adds a white dot and the previous white dot changes to black

Example 4 for Q21-25

Codes: The letters in the boxes all have a different meaning. The letters on the top are all related while the letters on the bottom have a different meaning but are related to one another. Work out what the different letters mean then work out the correct code for the given shape.

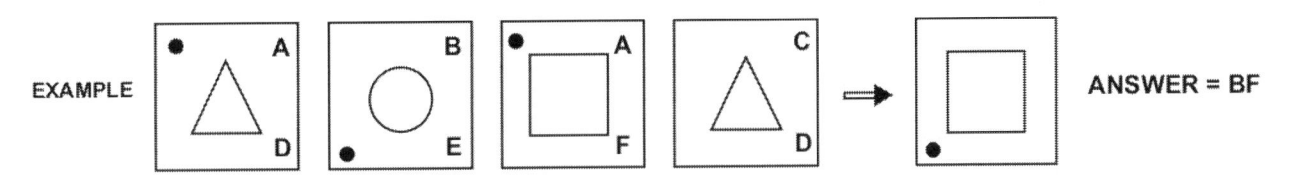

EXAMPLE

ANSWER = BF

A= Dot on top left   B= Dot on bottom left   C= No dot   D= Triangle   E= Circle   F= Square

Example 5 for Q26-30

Reflect the shape: Work out which picture is the exact reflection of the given shape in the mirror line.

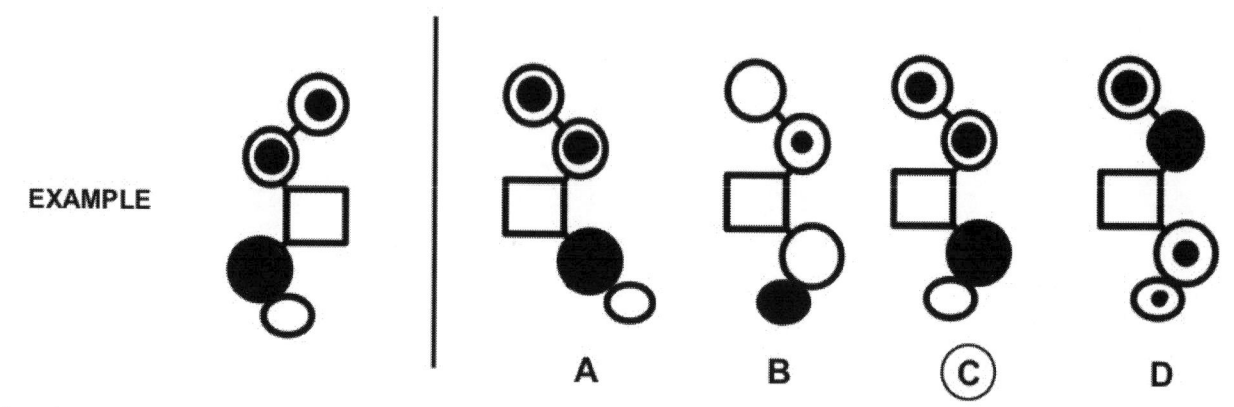

EXAMPLE

A   B   C   D

C is the correct answer because you have to reflect the given shape directly into the black line which represents the mirror.

Section 2 : Non-verbal reasoning

What to do: read the questions carefully and then calculate the correct answer. For each section of this non-verbal reasoning test, work out the correct answer and write your answer in your answer grid.

There are 30 questions in 15 minutes

Q1-5 Changing shapes: Look at how the example shape changes. Now pick the shape which shows how the given shape would change in the same way.

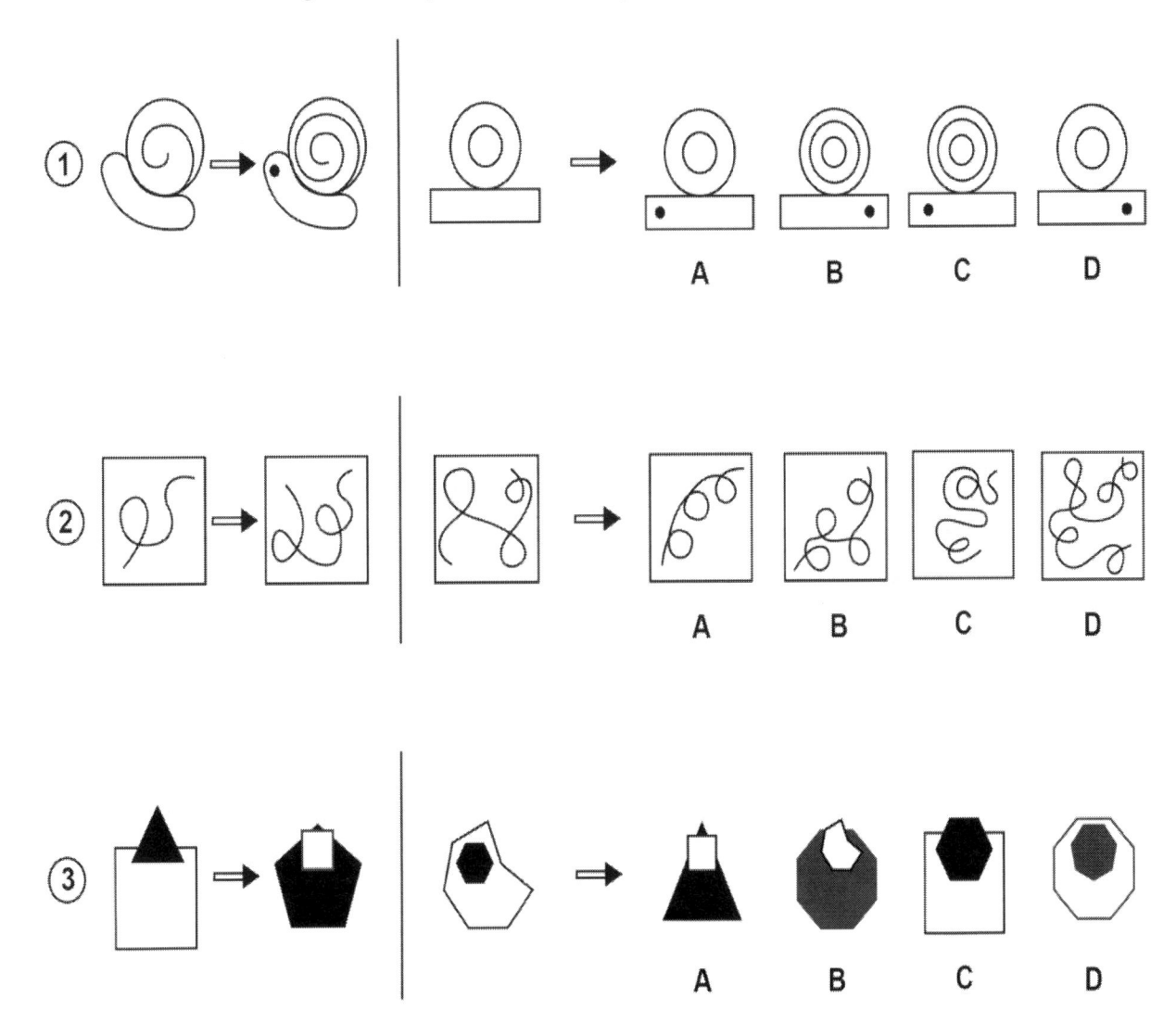

④

⑤

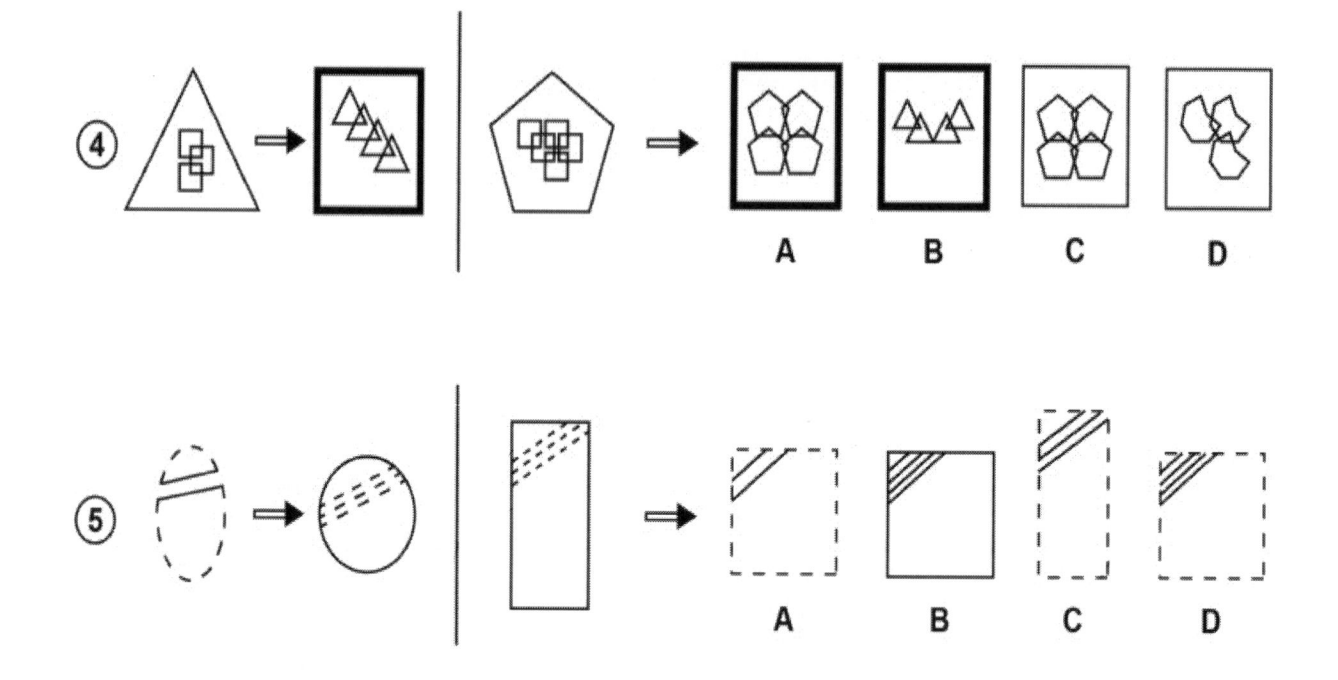

Q6-15 Cube nets: Work out which of the cubes is made from the net on the left.

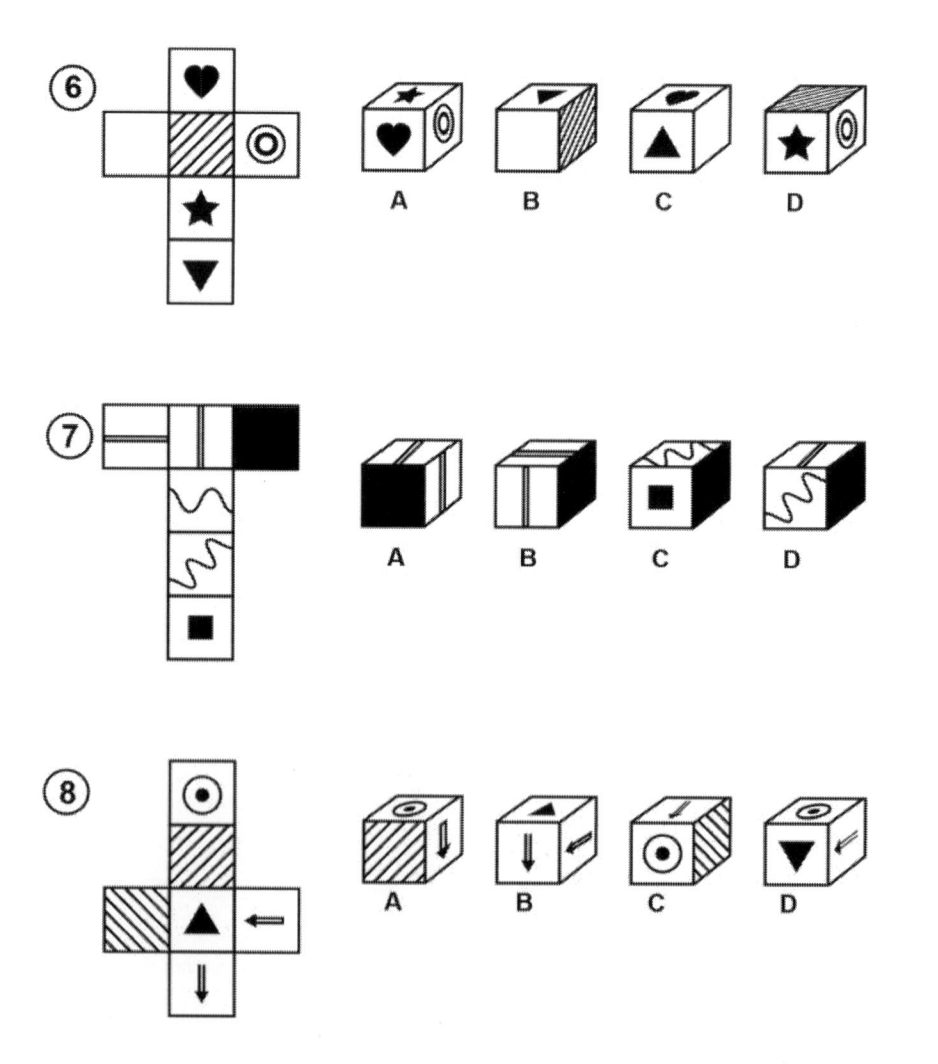

⑥

⑦

⑧

9.
10.
11.
12.
13.

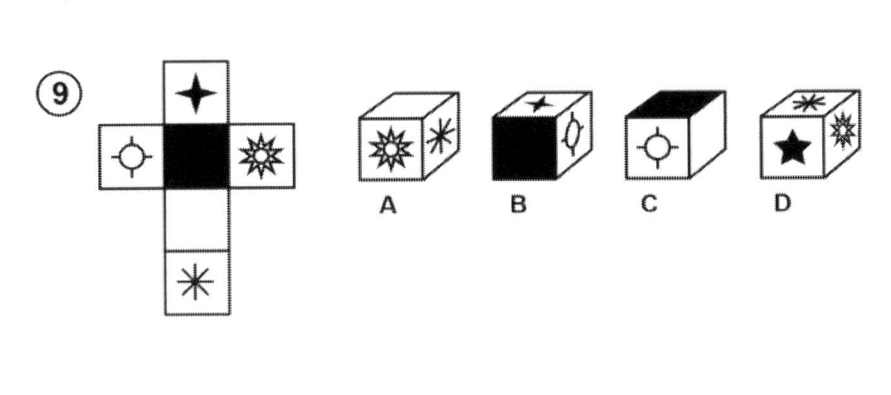

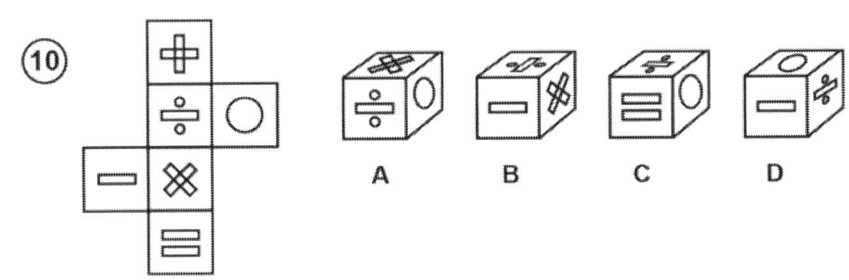

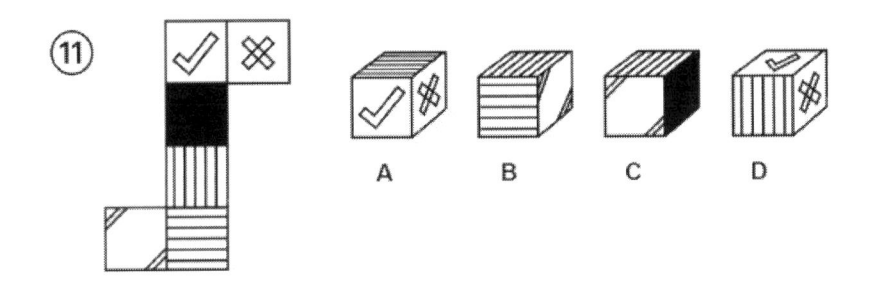

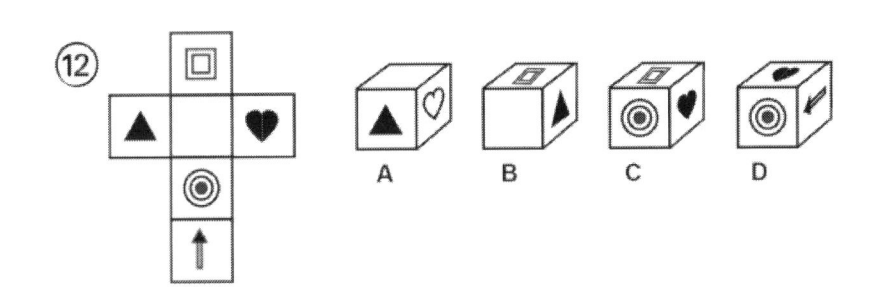

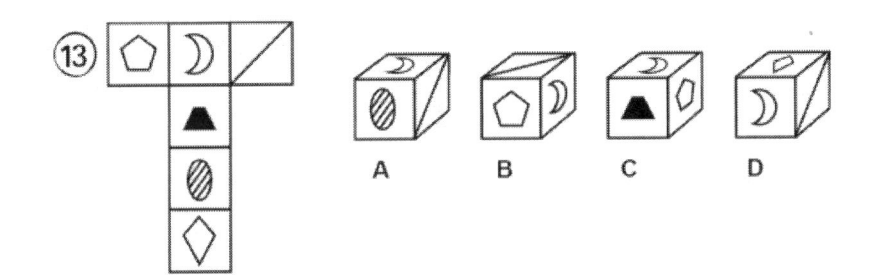

⑭

⑮

Q16-20

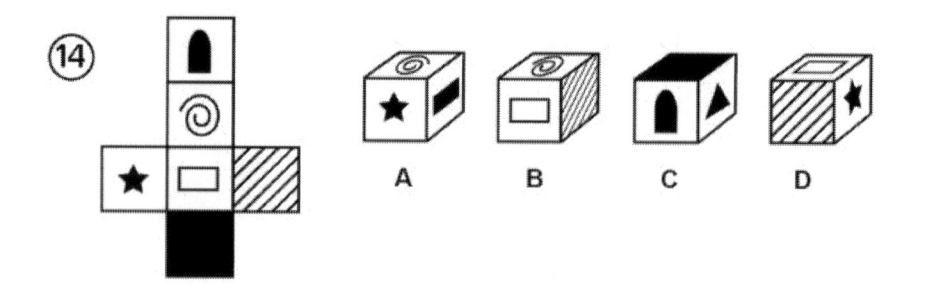

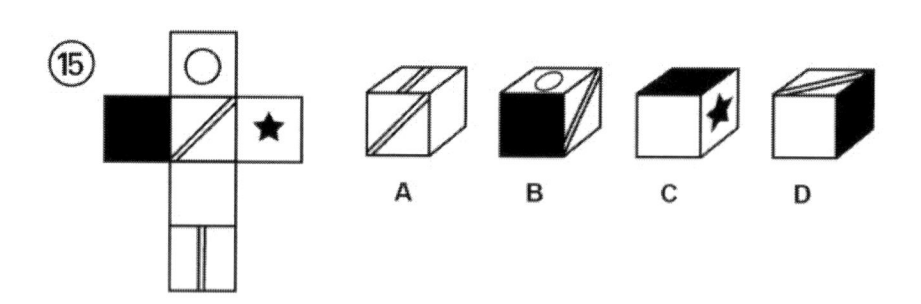

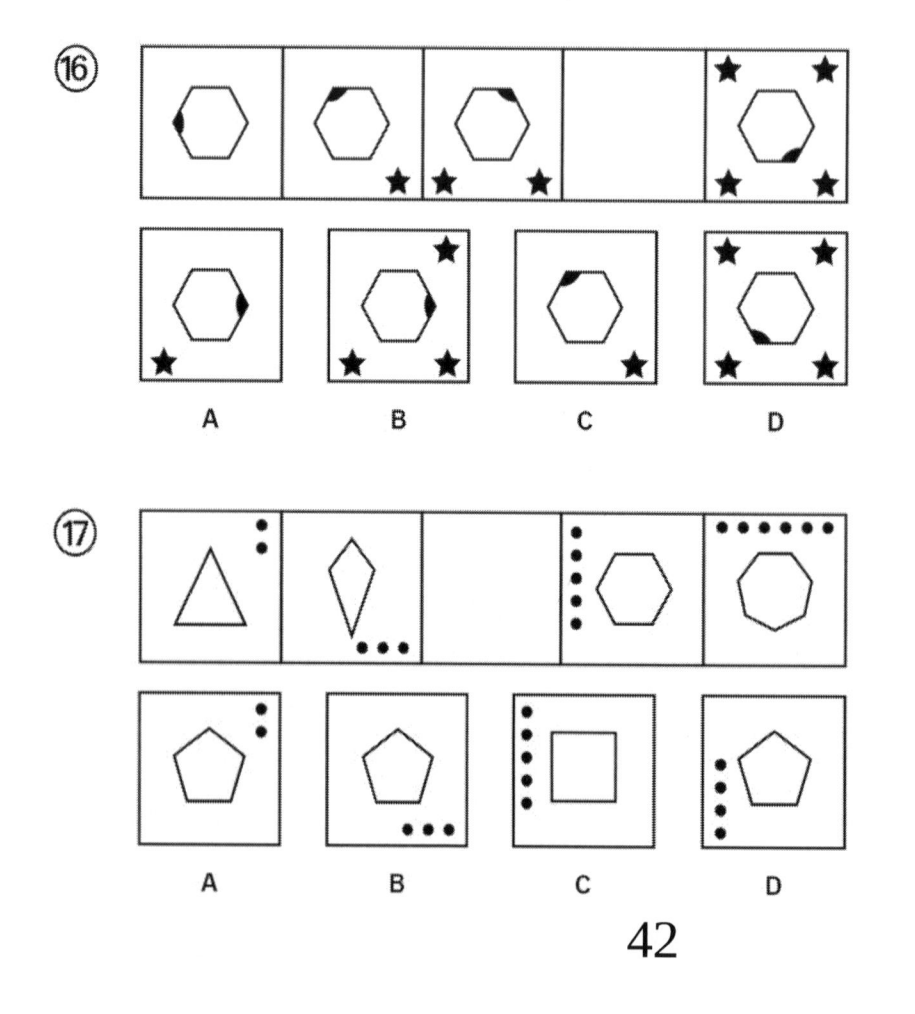

Complete the series: Work out which picture fits in the blank space.

⑯

⑰

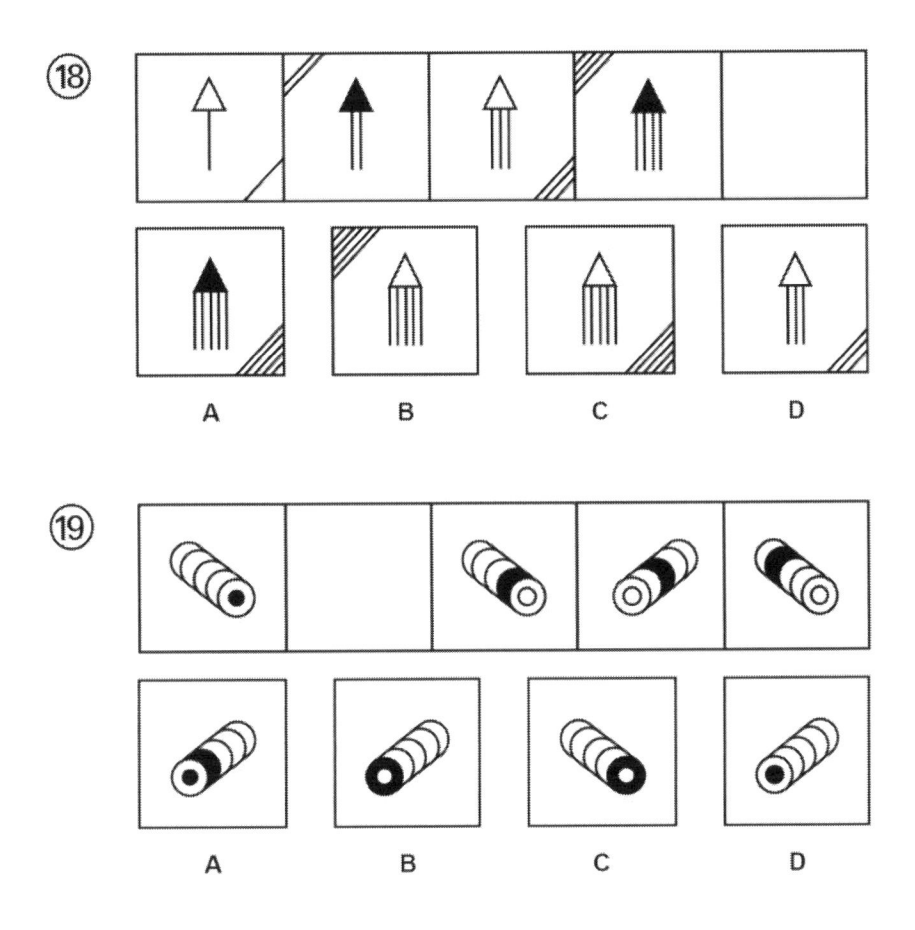

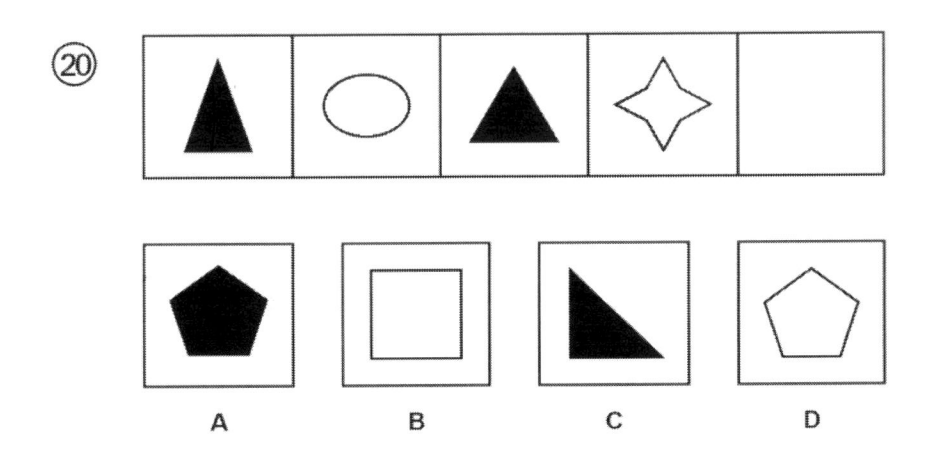

⑱

⑲

⑳

43

Q21-25

Codes: Work out what the different letters mean then work out the correct code for the given shape.

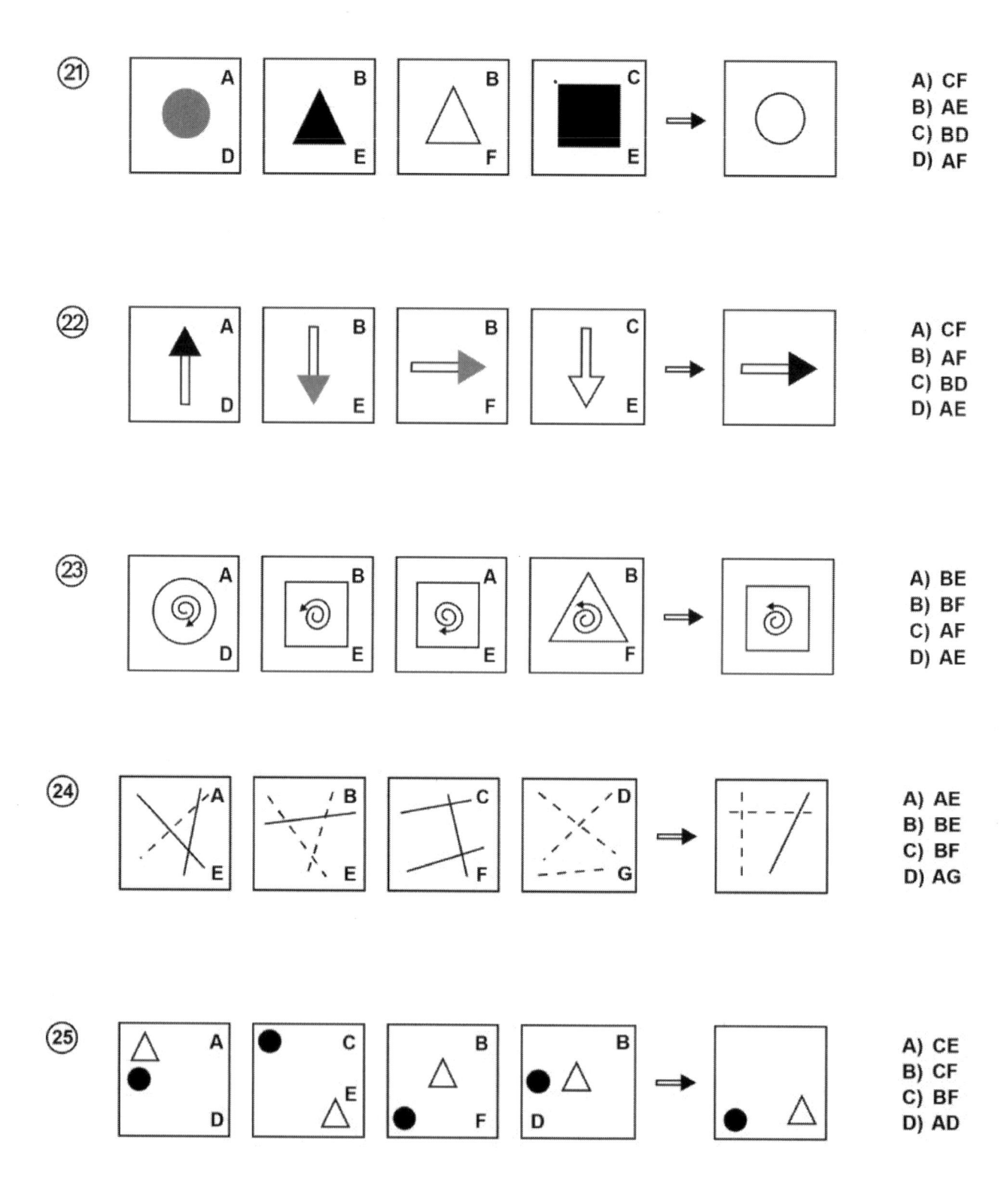

(21)
A) CF
B) AE
C) BD
D) AF

(22)
A) CF
B) AF
C) BD
D) AE

(23)
A) BE
B) BF
C) AF
D) AE

(24)
A) AE
B) BE
C) BF
D) AG

(25)
A) CE
B) CF
C) BF
D) AD

44

Q26-30

Reflect the shape: Work out which picture is the exact reflection of the given shape in the mirror line.

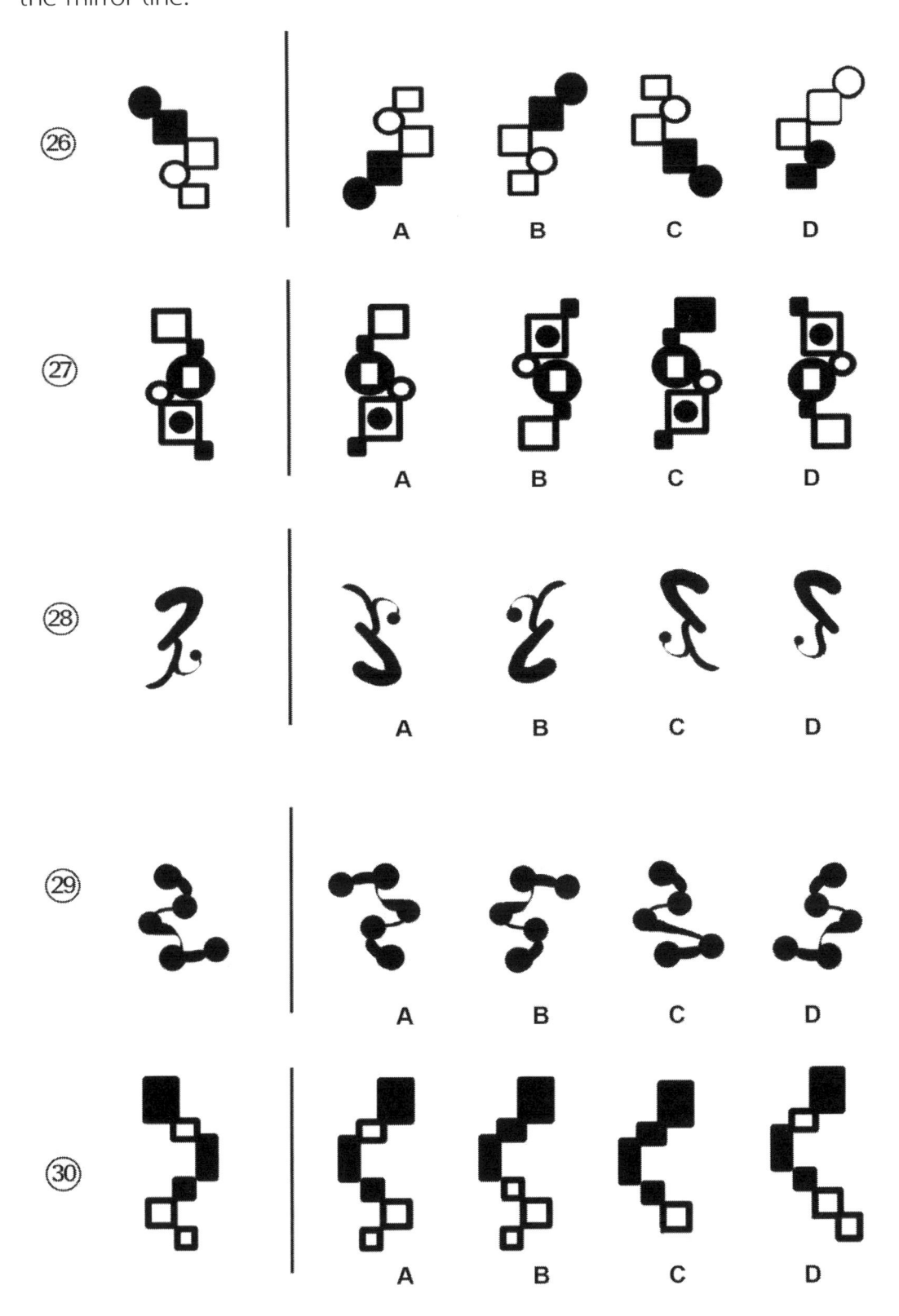

End of this section – Stop here .

End of this test paper.

Set B Paper 1

11+ CEM (Durham) Style Practice Paper

Gulliford Tutors

Copyright © Gulliford Tutors 2021
All rights reserved. No part of this book may be reproduced or transmitted in any form or by any means without written permission of the author.

Set B Paper 1

Instructions

1. You can use the question book to write on when working out answers.
2. Write your answers in the separate answer booklet provided. Mark your answer by drawing a line in the correct numbered box.

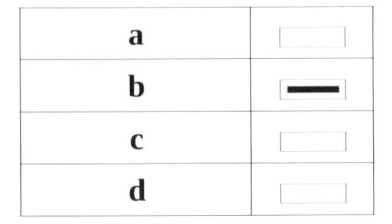

a	[ ]
b	[—]
c	[ ]
d	[ ]

3. If you need to write a number in the answer book, mark the digits in separate boxes.
4. Write in pencil only.
5. If you need to change your answer, make sure that you rub out the incorrect answer completely before writing in the new answer.
6. Answer as many questions as possible. If you have time left at the end of a section, go back and attempt any questions in that section which you left out before.
6. Do not move onto the next section until instructed to do so.
7. You will have 50 minutes to complete the whole paper, however each section has a time limit. You will be told the time limit at the start of each section.

Section 1 : Comprehension

Instructions on how to answer this section:

Read the passage of writing given to you then answer the questions writing the letter A,B,C or D corresponding to the correct answer on your answer sheet. Go back to the passage as many times as needed to find the answer.

Example:

Comets

Comets are small celestial bodies which orbit the Sun. They are mainly icy blocks made from frozen ammonia, methane and water and only contain a small amount of rock. Due to this, they are often nick-named 'dirty snowballs'.

Comets are made up of four components: the nucleus. Coma, dust trail and ion trail. The nucleus is made up of rocky material and can have a diameter of anything between 10 km and 100km. The Coma is the cloud of gases which are vaporised as the nucleus is heated as it approaches the sun. These gases are usually a mixture of water vapour, ammonia, carbon dioxide. The trails are tiny dust particles blown away as the nucleus heats and ionised gases are blown away from the Sun.

1. What is the Coma of a comet?
a. Rocky material and dust
b. A cloud of gases
c. A mixture of oxygen and carbon dioxide
d. A trail of ions

The correct answer is b a cloud of gases. Therefore you would put a line through the b box on Q1.

Section 1 : Comprehension

There are 12 questions in 10 minutes

What to do: read this passage carefully and then answer the questions.

The History of Gulliford Dissenters' Burial Ground

Gulliford Burial Ground is a tranquil and beautiful little graveyard hidden at the edge of the coastal village of Lympstone in Devon. For many years, this secret gem lay overgrown and forgotten until the two parishes and the newly formed Friends of Gulliford decided it was time to save such an important part of local and national history.

Before we come onto the story of Gulliford we need to set the scene. Let's go back four centuries to a time when everyone went to church on Sunday and not only that, but they were told which church they should attend which was usually their parish church. Oliver Cromwell and the Commonwealth were ruling the country and without the monarch as head of the Church of England, the established church was powerless to stop the rise of dissenters or non-conformists as they are also known. They were dissenting against the Church of England ; they wanted to distance themselves from the rituals and finery, bringing religion back to a simpler faith & life style.

With the return of Charles II to the throne, life once more became difficult for the dissenters. Charles needed to take back control as the Head of the Church of England, handing out death warrants to dissenting hard liners. Dissenter preachers were compelled to give their services in secret in people's homes and often there would be a hiding place for the minister to go in if soldiers raided the house.

In 1689 King William and Queen Mary decreed that dissenters could build their own chapels so they could worship openly. Mr Thomas Lee donated a corner of his field for a chapel. This became the Gulliford Chapel. People came from all the villages and towns in the vicinity. The chapel would have been very plain and frugal with no stained glass windows, paintings or gold ornaments. It would have consisted of just wooden pews to sit on, a pulpit for the minister to preach from and some musical instruments to accompany hymns.

However the congregation grew to over 300 so that a new , bigger chapel was needed. In 1774, this was completed. However, By the mid 19th century there was a decline in numbers of worshippers, brought on by the elderly dying and many more non-conformers' chapels being built in the surrounding area. Gulliford needed the money a congregation generated from subscriptions so ,as the numbers diminished, it was not possible to pay for the upkeep of the site. In 1907 the chapel roof was precarious and the walls needed strengthening, the cost of repair was deemed unaffordable and the decision to demolish the chapel at a cost of £20 was taken. With the chapel gone and only a few of the congregation left, the site was abandoned and slowly became overgrown and forgotten for the next few decades.

Then in 1993, Woodbury & Lympstone Parish Councils negotiated the purchase & management of Gulliford. Many years of hard work followed: laying a new path, repairing the wall facing the road, new gates, a bench, an information board and placing the stone ball back up on its plinth, Gulliford was finally re-opened much to the delight of the locals and again, a part of the local history was accessible to all.

1. Where is the Dissenters' Burial ground located?

a. In Cornwall

b. On the moors

c. Near the sea

d. Outside the town of Lynton in Devon

2. What does 'tranquil' mean?

a. Overgrown

b. Peaceful

c. Hidden away

d. Relaxed

3. How many years in 'four centuries'?

a. 4

b. 40

c. 400

d. 4000

4. Why did Cromwell and the church have difficulty controlling dissenters?

a. There was no King or Queen

b. The commonwealth followed different religions

c. No-one liked their parish church

d. most people were poor

5. How did Charles II try to ban dissenters?

a. He became head of the Church of England

b. He banned services in homes

c. His soldiers made people go to the parish church

d. He ordered those who continued to preach to be executed

6. What were dissenter chapels like?

a. Beautiful and full of stained glass

b. simple and unadorned

c. Empty other than church benches

d. In the countryside

7. What does the phrase 'in the vicinity' mean?

a. In the city area

b. Out of the parish

c. in the country

d. In the local area

8. Why did the chapel struggle to have enough finance?

a. There were less and less worshippers

b. They had to spend it all on repairs

c. People now wanted chapels with paintings and gold

d. The subscriptions weren't high enough9. What does 'congregation' mean?

9. What does 'congregation' mean?

a. The choir that sings in the church or chapel

b. A crowd of people

c. Local residents

d. The people who go to the church or chapel

10. What was wrong with the chapel roof?

a. It let in rain

b. it needed new tiles

c. It was dangerous and likely to collapse

d. People came to look at it

11. Why were they called 'dissenters or non-conformists' ?

a. They were never happy

b. They conformed to the rules of the Church of England

c. They would not follow the rules of the Church of England

d. They like singing their own hymns

12. What does ' accessible to all' mean?

a. Everyone can go into the site

b. Local history has been highlighted in a book

c. It is disability friendly

d. You have to pay an entry fee

> End of this section – Stop here .

Section 2 : Odd one out

Instructions on how to answer this section:

Each question has four words. Three of them are linked in some way and one is the odd one out. You must find the odd one out and mark it in your answer booklet.

e.g.   a. cheese   b. butter   c. yoghurt   d. <u>cake</u>

The answer is d. cake is the odd one out as the others are made from milk.

Section 2 : Odd one out

What to do: Find the odd one out in each group and mark it in the answer booklet.

There are 20 questions in 7 minutes

1)	a. career	b. stroll	c. saunter	d. amble
2)	a. advantage	b. benefit	c. hindrance	d. gain
3)	a. conclusion	b. finish	c. end	d. start
4)	a. confused	b. perplexed	c. bewildered	d. clear
5)	a. erratic	b. uniform	c. consistent	d. organised
6)	a. infuriated	b. angry	c. forbearing	d. enraged
7)	a. assiduous	b. indifferent	c. diligent	d. scrupulous
8)	a. lethargic	b. lively	c. listless	d. fatigued
9)	a. courage	b. fortitude	c. audacity	d. cowardice
10)	a. traditional	b. customary	c. unorthodox	d. conventional
11)	a. dispute	b. concur	c. agree	d. consent
12)	a. ambiguous	b. vague	c. definite	d. uncertain
13)	a. heartened	b. gloomy	c. melancholy	d. despondent
14)	a. convoluted	b. evident	c. complex	d. complicated
15)	a. anonymous	b. incognito	c. unidentified	d. known
16)	a. spurs	b. boosts	c. encourages	d. represses

17) a. wholesome b. unhealthy c. nutritious d. beneficial

18) a. allocation b. fraction c. portion d. entirety

19) a. critical b. superficial c. irrelevant d. trivial

20) a. square b. rectangle c. trapezium d. pentagon

End of this section – Stop here .

Section 3 : Antonyms

Instructions on how to answer this section:

An Antonym is a word with the opposite or nearly opposite meaning to another word. In this section, you need to work out the antonym of the given word. Once you have found the antonym, you must then mark it in your answer booklet.

Eg Large   a. enormous   b. wide   c. flamboyant   d. small

The answer is d. small because it has the opposite meaning to large.

Section 3 : Antonyms

What to do: Work out the antonym (word meaning the opposite) of the given word and mark your answer in the answer grid.

> There are 20 questions in 9 minutes

1)	**liberty**	a. freedom	b. liberal	c. captivity	d. prisoner
2)	**serene**	a. frenzied	b. calm	c. serious	d. satisfied
3)	**provoke**	a. annoy	b. prove	c. audacious	d. pacify
4)	**accurate**	a. mismatched	b. inexact	c. mathematical	d. discord
5)	**careless**	a. fatigued	b. scrupulous	c. uncaring	d. diligent
6)	**deny**	a. incompetent	b. refuse	c. imagine	d. confess
7)	**variable**	a. mixed	b. straight	c. variety	d. constant
8)	**hostile**	a. enemy	b. horrible	c. amiable	d. colleague
9)	**conspicuous**	a. conspiring	b. famous	c. hidden	d. secret
10)	**beautiful**	a. grotesque	b. unique	c. lovely	d. pretty
11)	**seek**	a. hidden	b. search	c. follow	d. evade
12)	**gloomy**	a. pessimistic	b. optimistic	c. grumpy	d. malignant
13)	**reluctant**	a. lethargic	b. popular	c. unhappy	d. keen
14)	**loathe**	a. unruly	b. cherish	c. hate	d. villain

15) **conventional**   a. unique   b. traditional   c. routine   d. mediocre

16) **encourage**   a. support   b. bravery   c. deter   d. succeed

17) **shrink**   a. reduce   b. population   c. aggravate   d. elongate

18) **infamous**   a. celebrity   b. unknown   c. blatant   d. rich

19) **inhibit**   a. promote   b. obscure   c. shield   d. damage

20) **premeditated**   a. predicted   b. foremost   c. spontaneous   d. cure

End of this section – Stop here.

Section 4 : Synonyms – missing letters

Instructions on how to answer this section:

A synonym is a word with the same or nearly the same meaning as another word. In this section, you need to work out the synonym of the given word and fill in the missing letters. You must then mark the correct missing letters in your answer booklet.

Eg   Large   e[n]o r[m]o[u]s

Section 4 : Synonyms – missing letters

There are 18 questions in 10 minutes

What to do: In this section, you need to work out the synonym of the given word and fill in the missing letters. You must then mark the correct missing letters in your answer booklet.

1)   dusk   ☐ w ☐ l i ☐ ☐ t

2)   stiff   r ☐ g ☐ d

3)   inept   ☐ s e ☐ ☐ s s

4)   shy   b ☐ ☐ h f u l

5)   cease   t ☐ r ☐ i n ☐ ☐ e

6)   buys   ☐ u r c ☐ ☐ s ☐ s

7)   assist   s u ☐ p ☐ ☐ t

8)   toiled   w ☐ ☐ ☐ e d

9)	tedious	☐ o ☐ ☐ n g
10)	positive	☐ p ☐ i ☐ ☐ t i c
11)	occurring	☐ a p p ☐ ☐ i ☐ g
12)	revolves	r o ☐ ☐ t e s
13)	embellish	☐ ☐ c ☐ r ☐ t e
14)	substantial	☐ o n ☐ i ☐ e r ☐ ☐ e
15)	dangerous	☐ a z a r ☐ ☐ s
16)	noticeable	☐ ☐ n ☐ ☐ i c u ☐ u s
17)	need	r ☐ q ☐ ☐ r e
18)	adversary	o ☐ p o ☐ ☐ ☐ t

End of this section – Stop here .

Section 5 : Numerical Reasoning

Instructions on how to answer this section: In this mathematical section, you need to read the question and calculate the correct answer.

You will then need to write your answer in your answer grid. Firstly, write the answer in the space at the top of the grid, then you MUST write the individual digits in the column grid below, making sure that you mark each digit in the correct column grid for that specific question number.

What is 15% of 140?

The answer is 21.

Therefore write 21 in the space at the top of the grid and the digits 2 and 1 in the column grid as shown below.

2	1
0	0
1	1 ▬
2 ▬	2
3	3
4	4
5	5
6	6
7	7
8	8
9	9

Section 5 : Numerical Reasoning

What to do: read the questions carefully and then calculate the correct answer.

You will then need to write your answer in your answer grid. Firstly, write the answer in the space at the top of the grid, then you MUST write the individual digits in the column grid below, making sure that you mark each digit in the correct column grid for that specific question number.

There are 20 questions in 14 minutes

① What is 30% of 260 ?

② What is $\frac{5}{7}$ of 56 ?

③ ☐ + 232 = 768

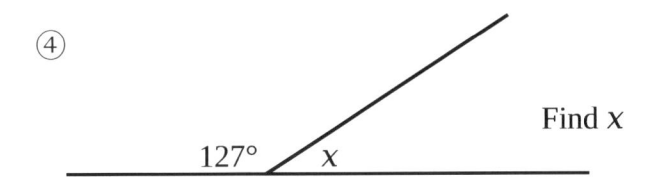

④ Find x (127°, x on a straight line)

⑤ $\frac{2}{3}$ of a number is 12. What is the number ?

⑥ £4.99 x 5 =

⑦ Peter pays for a book costing £15.95 with a £20 note. What change does he get ?

⑧ 7 x ☐ = 406

⑨ Round 4.583 to the nearest tenth.

⑩ 6a + 7 = 43   Find a .

⑪　Karl has 5 more cards than Joanne. If they have 29 cards in total, how many cards does Karl have?

⑫　Find the difference between 8^2 and 3^3.

⑬　30 – 8 x 2 + 4 =

⑭　If 64 x 18 = 1152
　　16 x 18 = ?

⑮　Find the largest number among:　2.473　2.47　2.528　1.715　1.7

⑯　What is half of 78 ?

⑰　Elliot gives 40% of his sweets to James. James gets 18 sweets. How many sweets did Elliot start with?

⑱　8, 4, 3, 3, 2　　Find the mean of these numbers.

⑲　The mean of 3 numbers is 31. If two of the numbers are 25 and 27, what is the last number ?

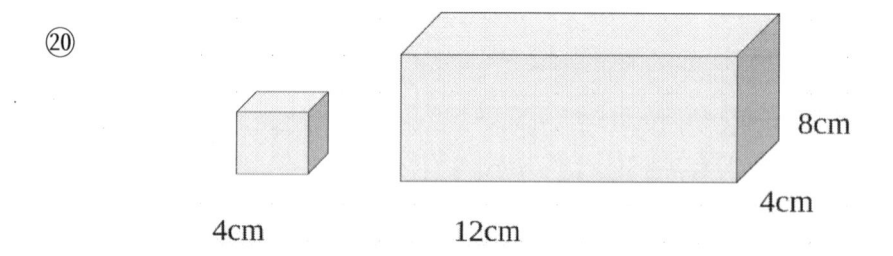

⑳　

4cm　　12cm　　　　8cm　　4cm

How many of the small cubes can fit into the large cuboid ?

End of this section – Stop here .

End of this test paper.

Set B Paper 2

11+ CEM (Durham) Style Practice Paper

Gulliford Tutors

Copyright © Gulliford Tutors 2021
All rights reserved. No part of this book may be reproduced or transmitted in any form or by any means without written permission of the author.

Set B paper 2

Instructions

1. You can use the question book to write on when working out answers.
2. Write your answers in the separate answer booklet provided. Mark your answer by drawing a line in the correct numbered box.

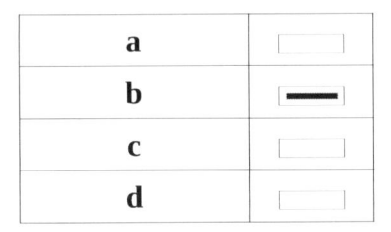

a	
b	—
c	
d	

3. If you need to write a number in the answer book, mark the digits in separate boxes.
4. Write in pencil only.
5. If you need to change your answer, make sure that you rub out the incorrect answer completely before writing in the new answer.
6. Answer as many questions as possible. If you have time left at the end of a section, go back and attempt any questions in that section which you left out before.
6. Do not move onto the next section until instructed to do so.
7. You will have 50 minutes to complete the whole paper, however each section has a time limit. You will be told the time limit at the start of each section.

Section 1 : Numerical Reasoning

Instructions on how to answer this section: In this mathematical section, you need to read the question and calculate the correct answer.

You will then need to write your answer in your answer grid. Firstly, write the answer in the space at the top of the grid, then you MUST write the individual digits in the column grid below, making sure that you mark each digit in the correct column grid for that specific question number.

What is 15% of 140?

The answer is 21.

Therefore write 21 in the space at the top of the grid and the digits 2 and 1 in the column grid as shown below.

2	1
0	0
1	1 ▬
2 ▬	2
3	3
4	4
5	5
6	6
7	7
8	8
9	9

Section 1 : Numerical Reasoning

What to do: read the questions carefully and then calculate the correct answer.

You will then need to write your answer in your answer grid. Firstly, write the answer in the space at the top of the grid, then you MUST write the individual digits in the column grid below, making sure that you mark each digit in the correct column grid for that specific question number.

> There are 40 questions in 35 minutes

① Jane has her 53rd birthday today. How many months old is she?

② Karen buys 3 swedes, 2 cabbages and 2 broccoli. How much does she pay in total?

Swede 48p
Parsnips 15p
Broccoli 54p
Cabbages 99p

③ Which is larger $\frac{5}{8}$ or $\frac{7}{9}$?

④ In a basket there are 3 apples, 5 oranges and 4 bananas. What is the probability of picking a banana?

⑤ Bill and Ted's ages total 90. If Bill is 6 years older than Ted. How old is Bill?

⑥ A car showroom surveys the numbers of cars it sell and draws a bar chart.

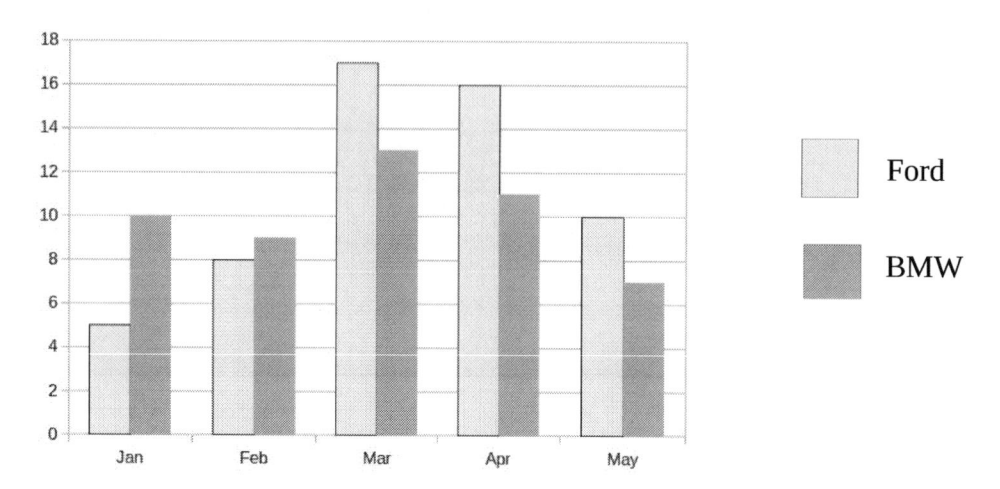

a) Which car was sold most?

b) During how many months did they sell over ten BMWs?

c) During which month did they sell twice as many BMWs than Fords?

d) How many Fords did they sell in total?

⑦ $\frac{1}{5}$, 0.23, 0.3, 27%, $\frac{1}{4}$. What number is the median?

⑧ In a school of 480 children, 95% eat school meals. How many don't eat school meals?

⑨ A cuboid box holds smaller 3cm cubes in it. The box is 12cm x 24cm x 18cm. How many cubes will fit in it?

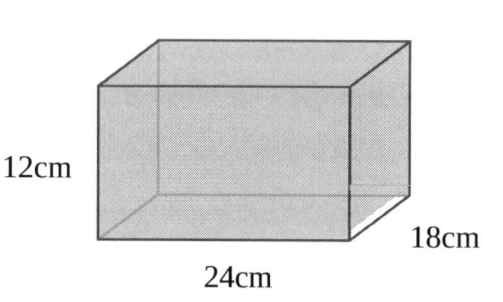

⑩ The square ABCD has been drawn on the graph. What are the coordinates of C?

⑪ Patrick has used 70% of his holiday money. He has £36 left. How much holiday money did he have in total?

⑫ Poonam wants to pave the area around her fish pond. How much will her slabs cost?

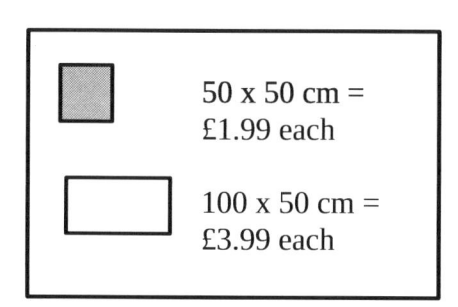

50 x 50 cm = £1.99 each

100 x 50 cm = £3.99 each

⑬

Number of spots	Number of ladybirds
1	🐞 🐞
2	🐞 🐞
3	🐞 🐞
4	🐞 🐞 🐞
5	🐞 🐞 🐞 🐞 🐞
6	🐞 🐞 🐞

A Pictogram represents the number of spots found on each ladybird.

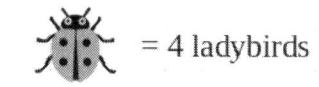

🐞 = 4 ladybirds

a) How many fewer ladybirds have 1 spot than 5 spots?

b) What is the mean number of ladybirds in each category?

c) What is the range of ladybirds in each category?

d) What percentage of ladybirds have 4 spots?

⑭   Children in a class were asked what pets they had. The results were put in a table.

	Dogs	Cats	Total
Black	17	15	
Not black	25	23	
Total			

a) How many dogs were there in the survey?

b) How many black cats were there in the survey?

c) How many animals altogether were there?

⑮

Dollars, $

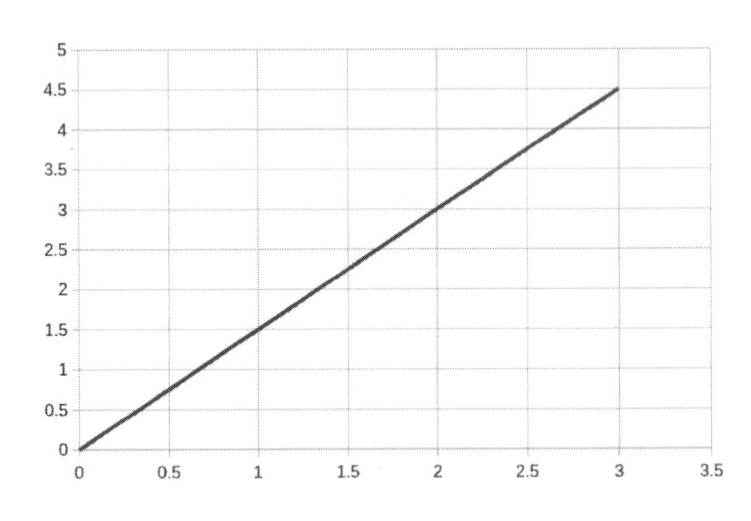

Pounds, £

Using the conversion graph above, answer the following questions:

a) Convert £2 into dollars.

b) A book costs $7.50. How much is this in pounds?

c) A belt costs $9. How much is this in pounds?

⑯   A sequence has numbers 2,5,8,11….

a) What is the 7th number in the sequence?

b) What is the formula of the sequence?

   a. 3n   b. n + 3   c. 3n – 1   d. 3n + 2

⑰ There are 320 roses in a rose garden. The pie chart shows the proportion of each colour of rose.

a) Which colour rose is there most of?

b) How many white roses are there?

c) One fifth of the roses are orange. How many orange roses are there?

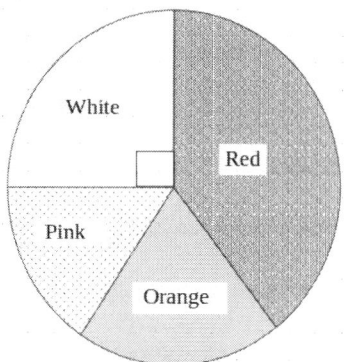

⑱ A bus stops outside your school every 20 minutes. The first bus each day stops at 8:10am and the last one stops at 9:50pm. How many buses stop there daily?

⑲

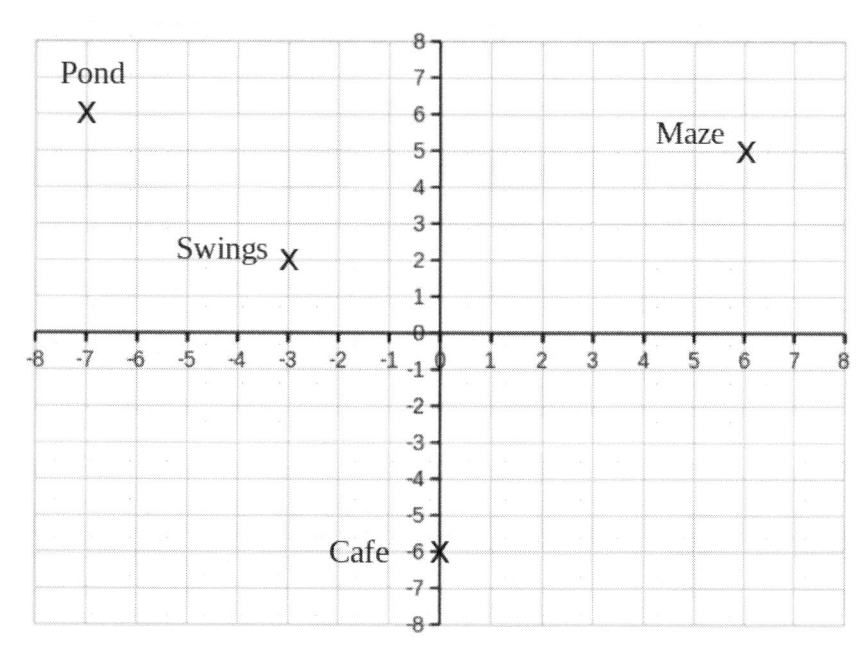

The grid shows the parts of the local park.

a) Give the co-ordinates of the cafe.

b) I'm facing North at the pond. What direction must I walk to get to the swings?

c) I'm at the maze and walk 4 squares South and 3 squares West. I'm now at the tennis courts. Give the co-ordinates of the tennis courts.

d) If I reflected the co-ordinates of the maze in the horizontal (x) axis, I find the cycle park. What are the co-ordinates of the cycle park?

20) Work out what order of rotational symmetry these shapes have.

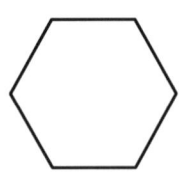

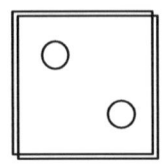

What is the sum of their orders of rotational symmetry?

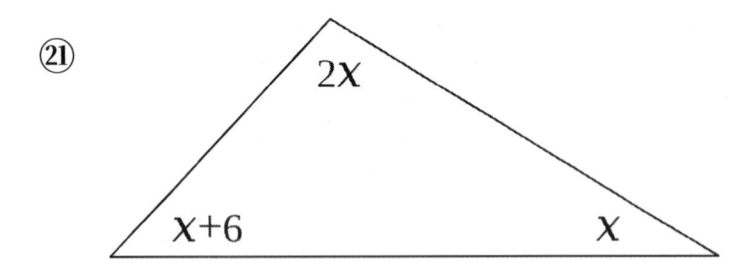

21)

Find the biggest angle in degrees.

22) Children at a club's swimming lessons were asked their favourite swim stroke. The table shows the answers in percentage.

Front crawl	42%
Breast stroke	24%
Back stroke	21%
Butterfly	3%
Doggie paddle	

a) What percentage of children like doggie paddle?

b) 300 children took part in the survey. How many children preferred backstroke?

c) Of the 300 children surveyed, $\frac{2}{3}$ of the children who liked front crawl were boys. How many boys liked front crawl?

End of this section – Stop here.

Section 2 : Non-verbal Reasoning

Instructions on how to answer this section: Look at each of the examples of how to solve these non-verbal reasoning questions. Each method is different so you must look at each example carefully.

Example 1 for Q1-5

Most like the first two: Look at the two examples given on the left. Work out what the left-hand shapes have in common. Now on the right-hand side of the line, work out which shape is most like the two example shapes.

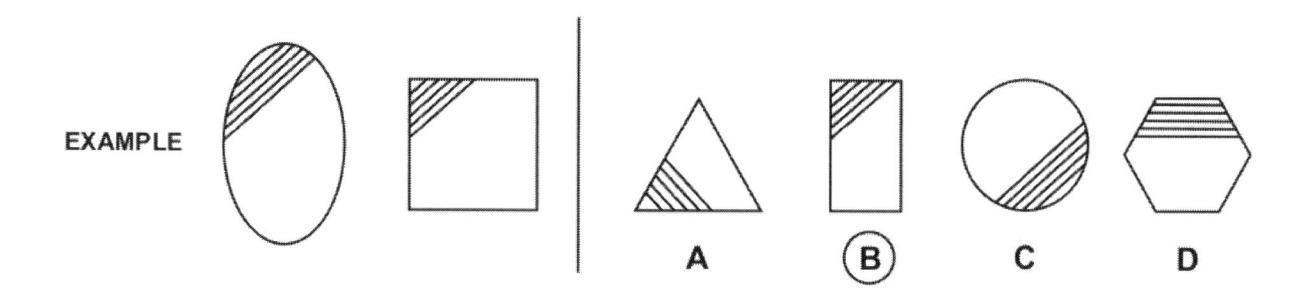

Example 2 for Q6-15

Cube nets: Look at the example given on the left. Work out which of the cubes is made from from cube net on the left.

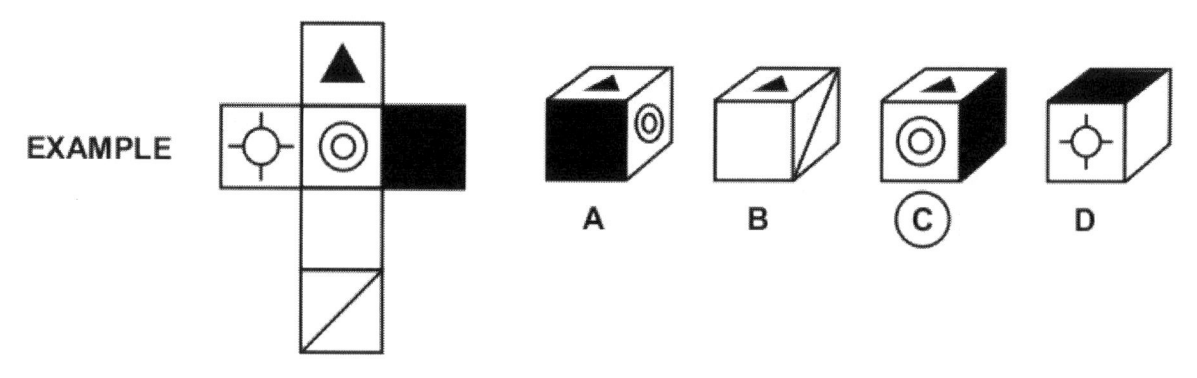

C is correct because on the net the triangle is directly above the double circle and the black is directly to the right of the double circle.

Example 3 for Q16-20

Rotations: Look at the example given on the left. It has been rotated. Work out which of the shapes on the right is the rotation of the example.

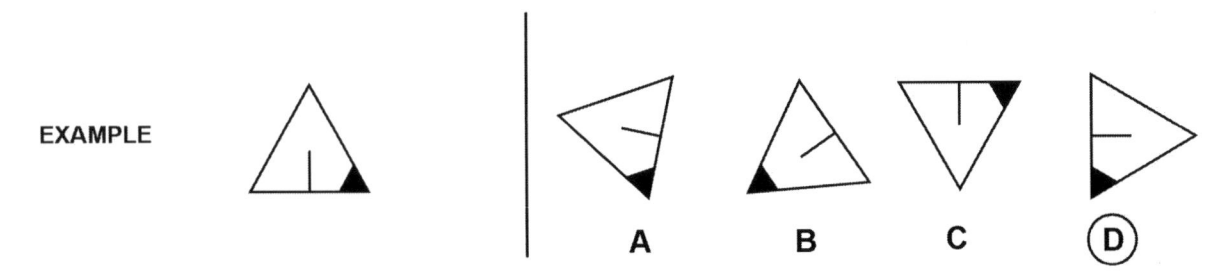

EXAMPLE

A   B   C   (D)

D is correct because it is identical to the given shape: it has the vertical line in the middle of the base and the black corner to the right of the vertical line.

Example 4 for Q21-25

Cube plans: If you looked directly down from the ceiling at the cube you would only see the 2-D floor plan. Work out which floor plan corresponds to the 3-D shape.

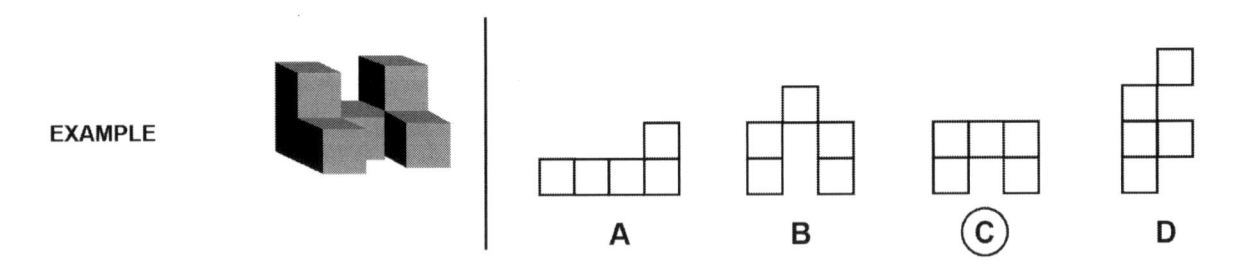

EXAMPLE

A   B   (C)   D

C is correct because it has the same floor plan as the given shape.

Example 5 for Q26-30

Odd one out: Three of the patterns have something in common. Work out which is the odd one out.

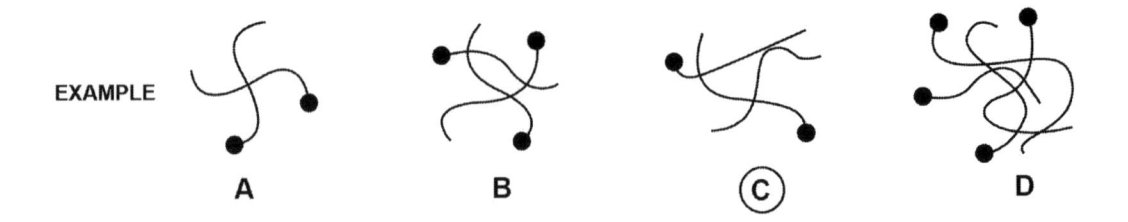

EXAMPLE

A   B   (C)   D

C is correct because the others have the same number of black dots as number of lines.

Section 2 : Non-verbal reasoning

What to do: read the questions carefully and then calculate the correct answer.

For each section of this non-verbal reasoning test, work out the correct answer and write your answer in your answer grid.

There are 30 questions in 15 minutes

Q1-10 Most like the first two: Look at the two examples given on the left. Work out what the left-hand shapes have in common. Now work out which shape is most like the two example shapes.

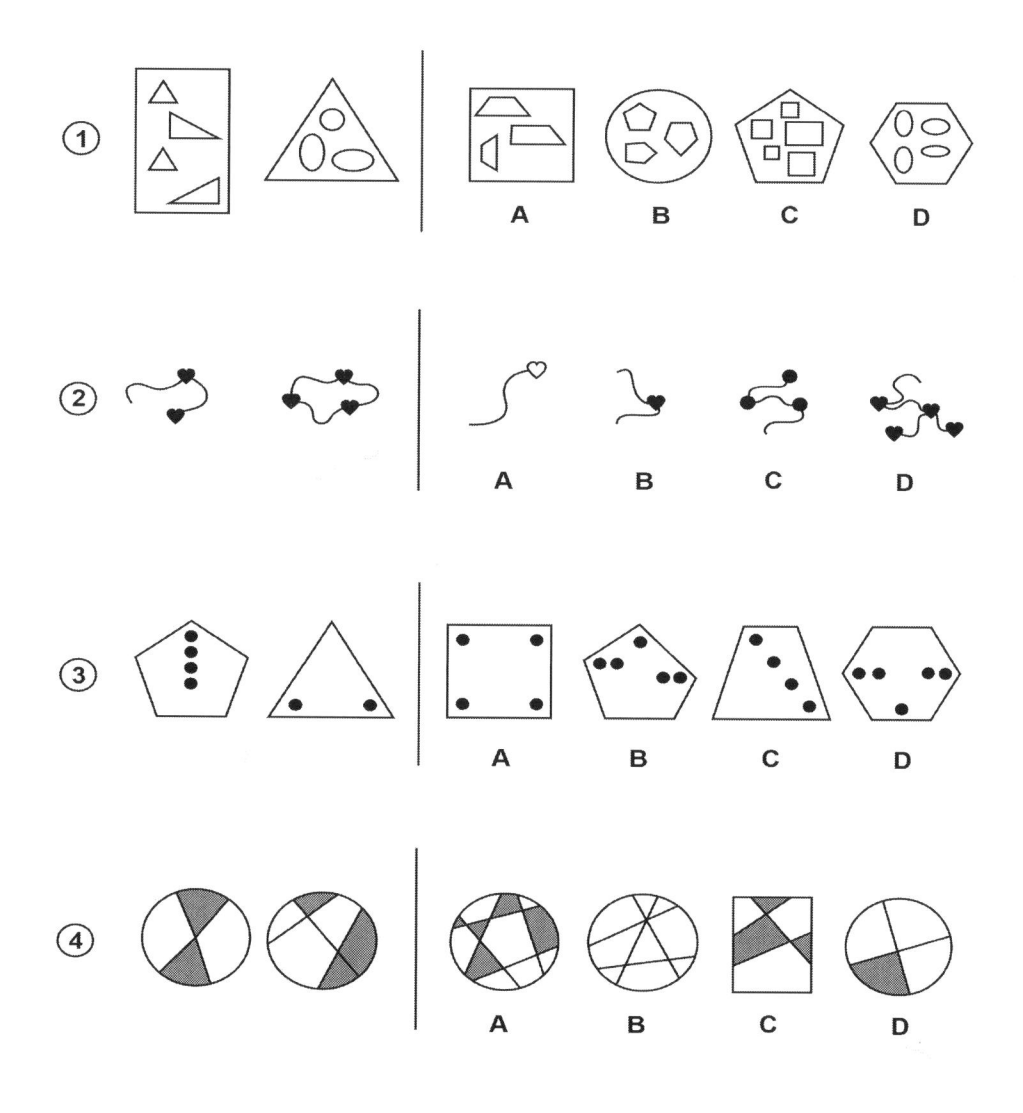

⑤ A B C D

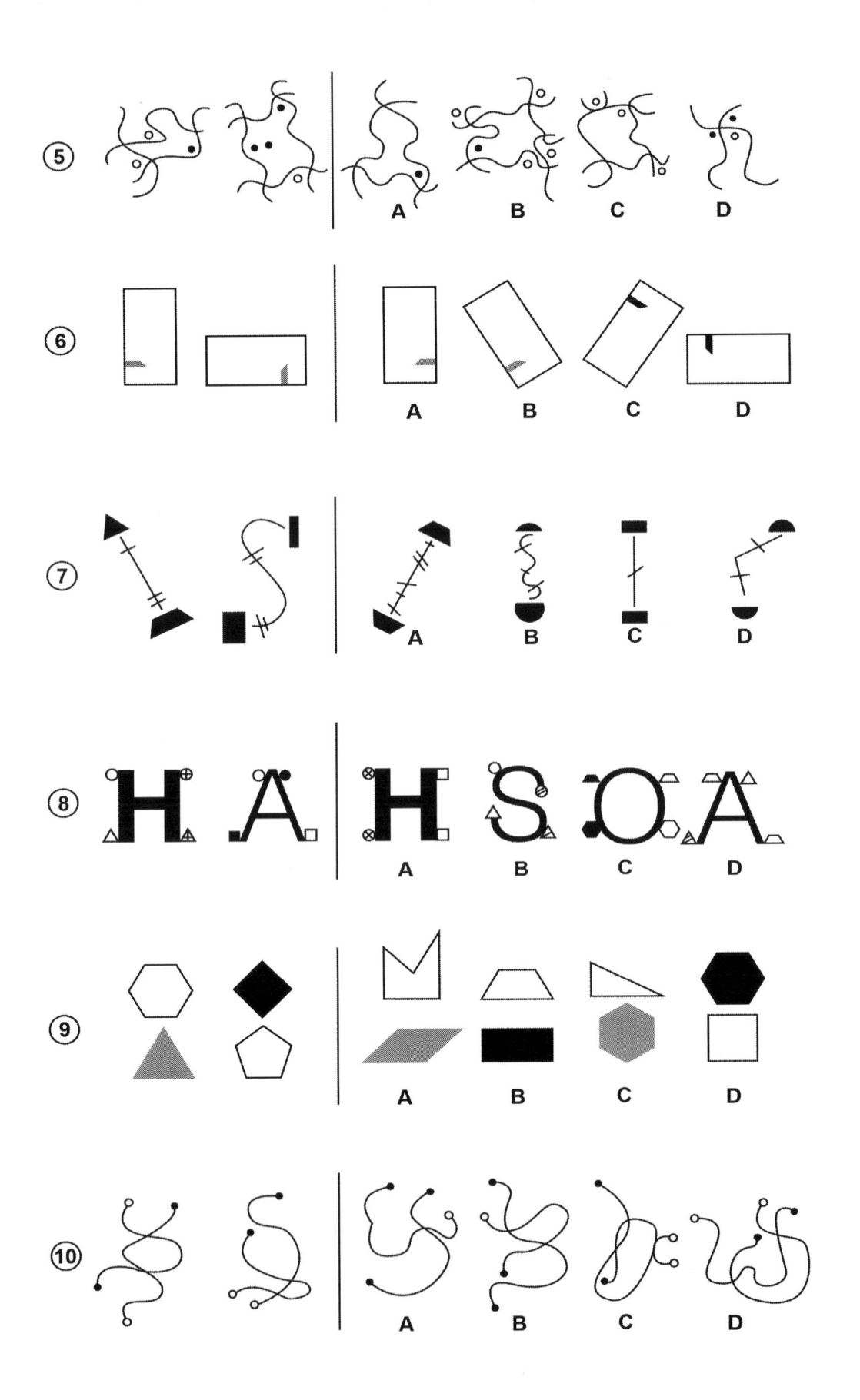

⑥ A B C D

⑦ A B C D

⑧ A B C D

⑨ A B C D

⑩ A B C D

82

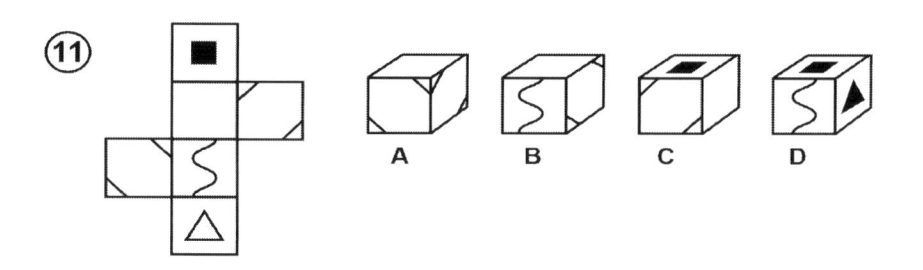

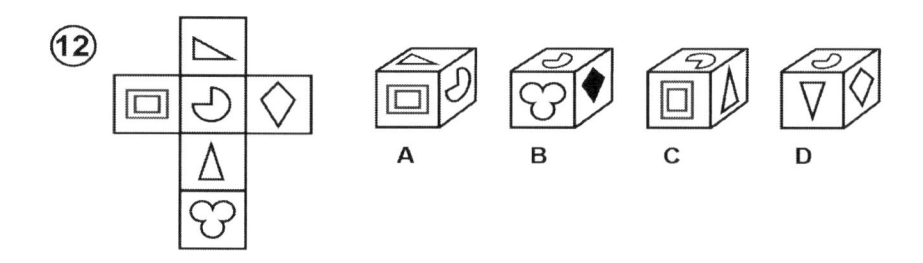

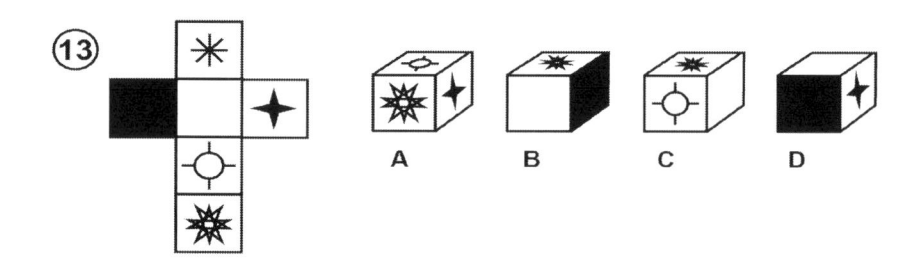

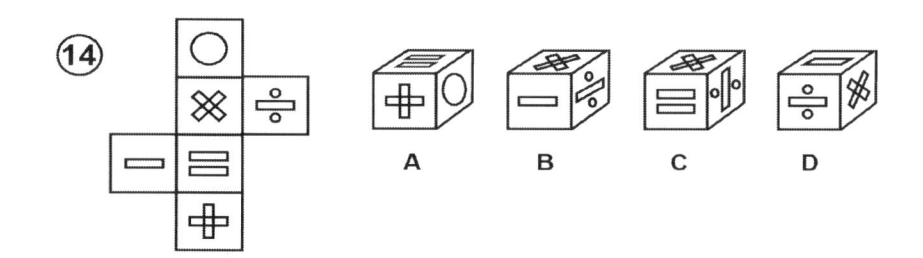

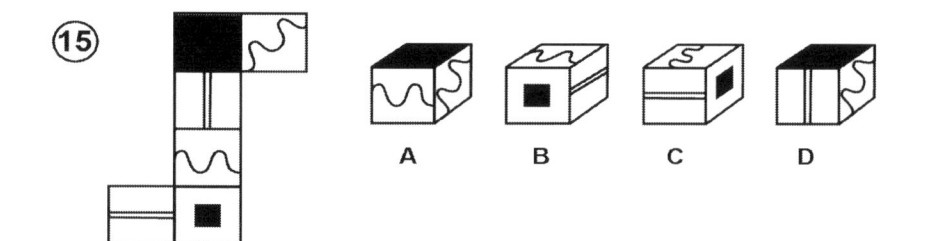

Q 11 – 15 Cube nets: Work out which of the cubes is made from the net on the left.

Q 16 – 20 Rotations: Work out which shape is obtained by rotating the shape on the left.

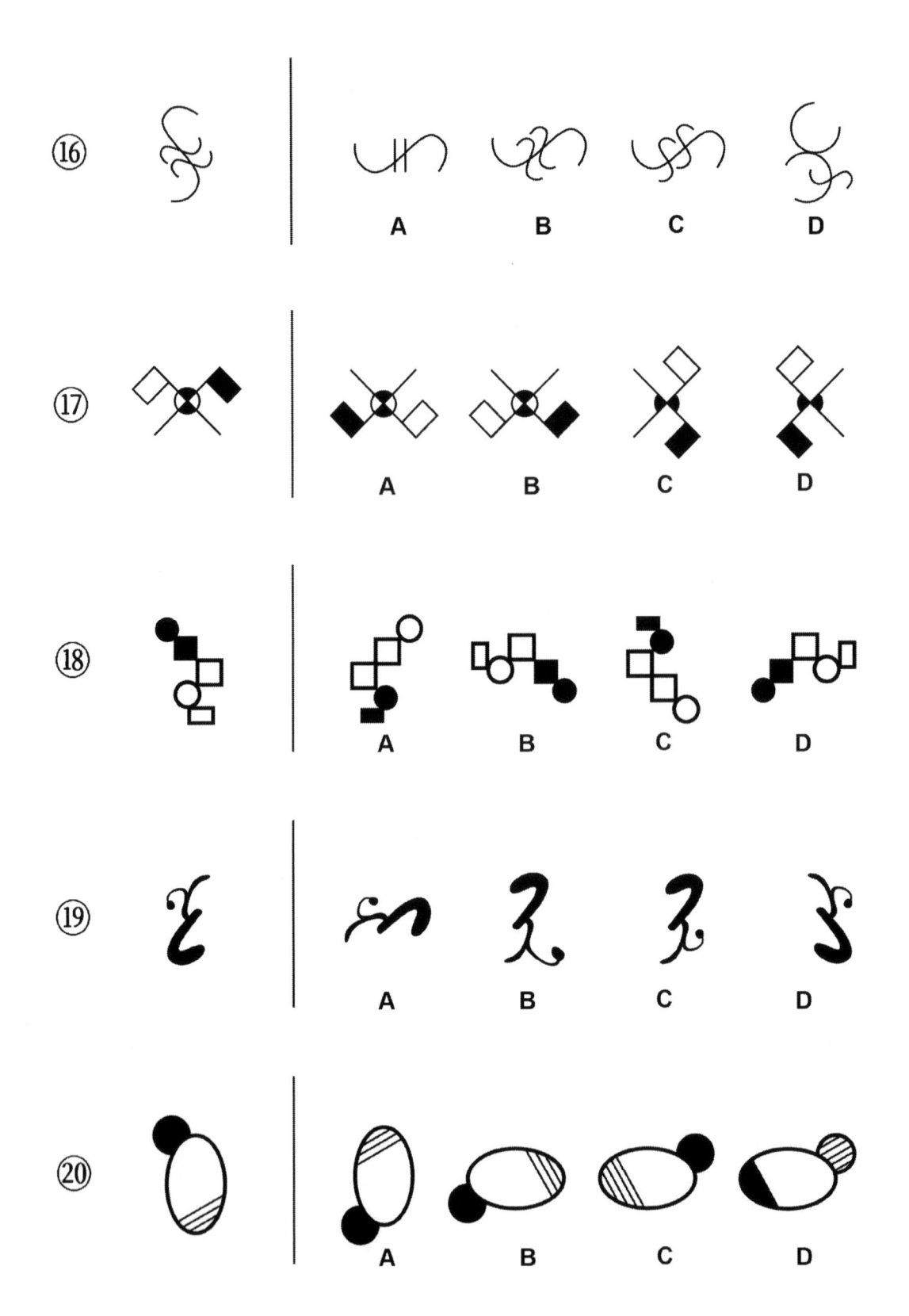

⑯

| | A | B | C | D |

⑰

| | A | B | C | D |

⑱

| | A | B | C | D |

⑲

| | A | B | C | D |

⑳

| | A | B | C | D |

84

Q 21 – 25 Cube plans.: Work out which of the 2-D cube plans corresponds to the 3-D shape.

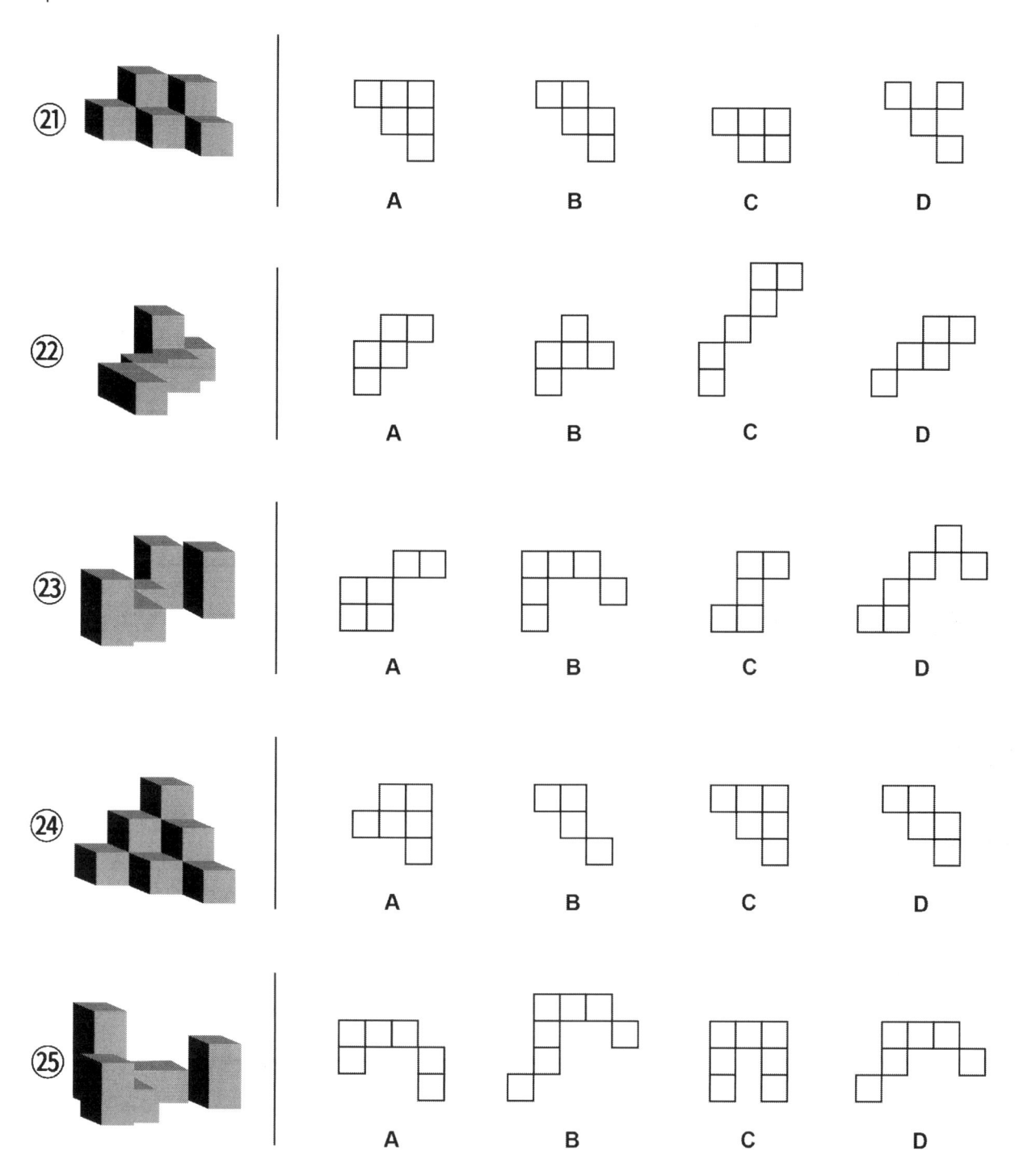

Q 26 – 30 Odd one out: Three of the shapes have something in common. Work out which is the odd one out.

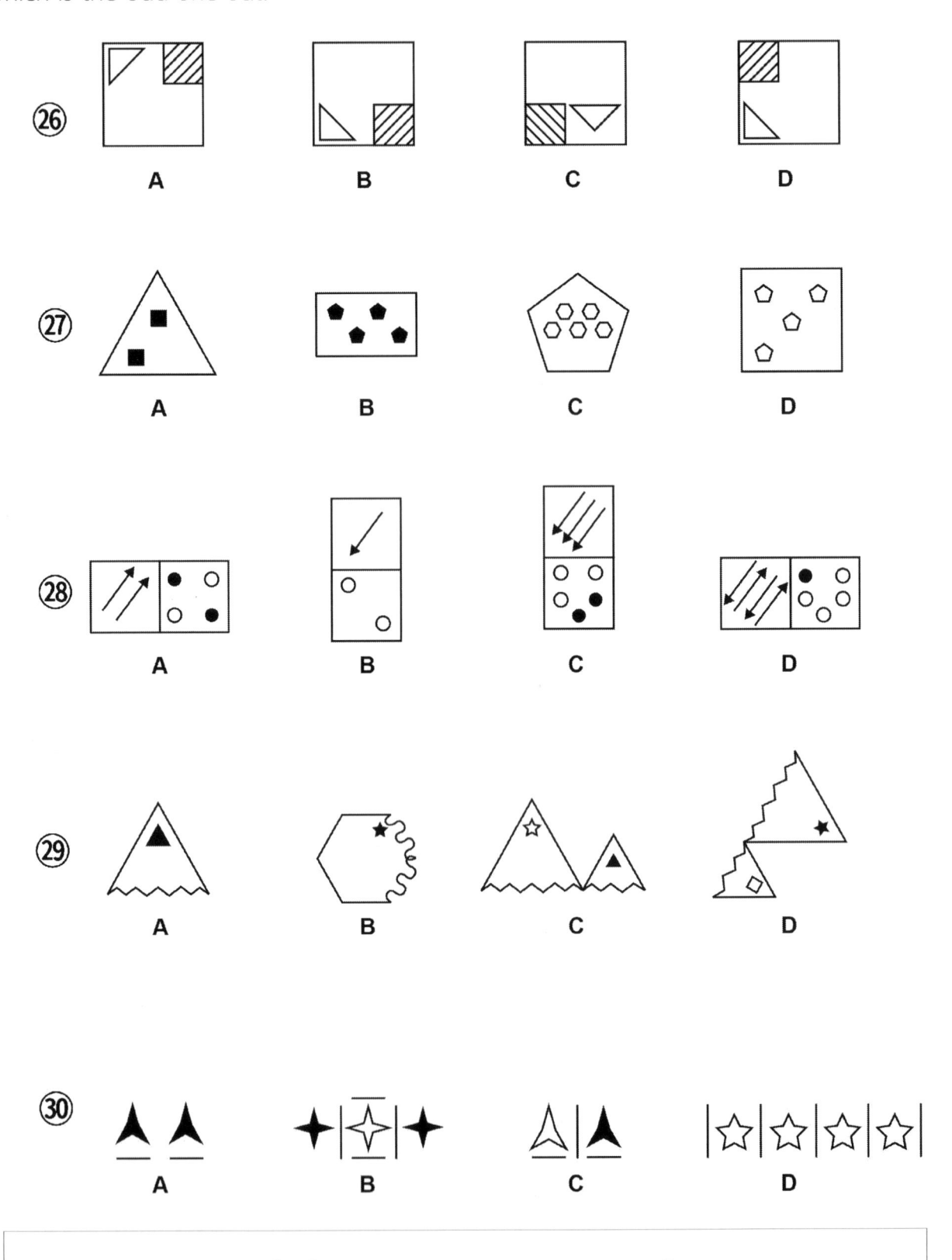

㉖   A   B   C   D

㉗   A   B   C   D

㉘   A   B   C   D

㉙   A   B   C   D

㉚   A   B   C   D

End of this section – Stop here .

End of test

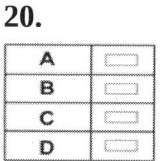

Set A Paper 1

Name:

Section 1 : Comprehension

1. A B C D
2. A B C D
3. A B C D
4. A B C D
5. A B C D
6. A B C D
7. A B C D
8. A B C D
9. A B C D
10. A B C D
11. A B C D
12. A B C D
13. A B C D
14. A B C D
15. A B C D

End of this section - Stop here.

Section 2 : Synonyms

1. A B C D
2. A B C D
3. A B C D
4. A B C D
5. A B C D
6. A B C D
7. A B C D
8. A B C D
9. A B C D
10. A B C D
11. A B C D
12. A B C D
13. A B C D
14. A B C D
15. A B C D
16. A B C D
17. A B C D
18. A B C D
19. A B C D
20. A B C D

End of this section - Stop here.

Set A Paper 1

Section 3 : CLOZE – Wordbank.

Aesop's Fables – The lion and the bull.

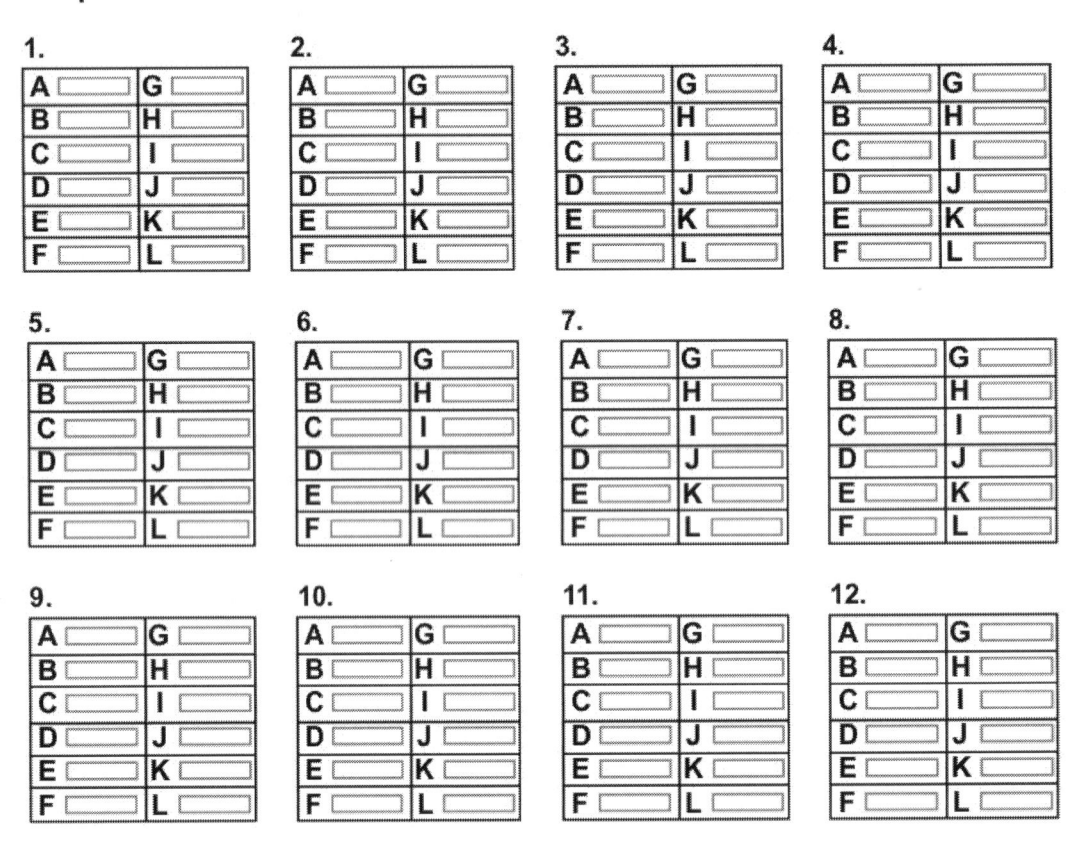

1.

A	G
B	H
C	I
D	J
E	K
F	L

2.

A	G
B	H
C	I
D	J
E	K
F	L

3.

A	G
B	H
C	I
D	J
E	K
F	L

4.

A	G
B	H
C	I
D	J
E	K
F	L

5.

A	G
B	H
C	I
D	J
E	K
F	L

6.

A	G
B	H
C	I
D	J
E	K
F	L

7.

A	G
B	H
C	I
D	J
E	K
F	L

8.

A	G
B	H
C	I
D	J
E	K
F	L

9.

A	G
B	H
C	I
D	J
E	K
F	L

10.

A	G
B	H
C	I
D	J
E	K
F	L

11.

A	G
B	H
C	I
D	J
E	K
F	L

12.

A	G
B	H
C	I
D	J
E	K
F	L

End of this section - Stop here.

Section 4 : Shuffled Sentences

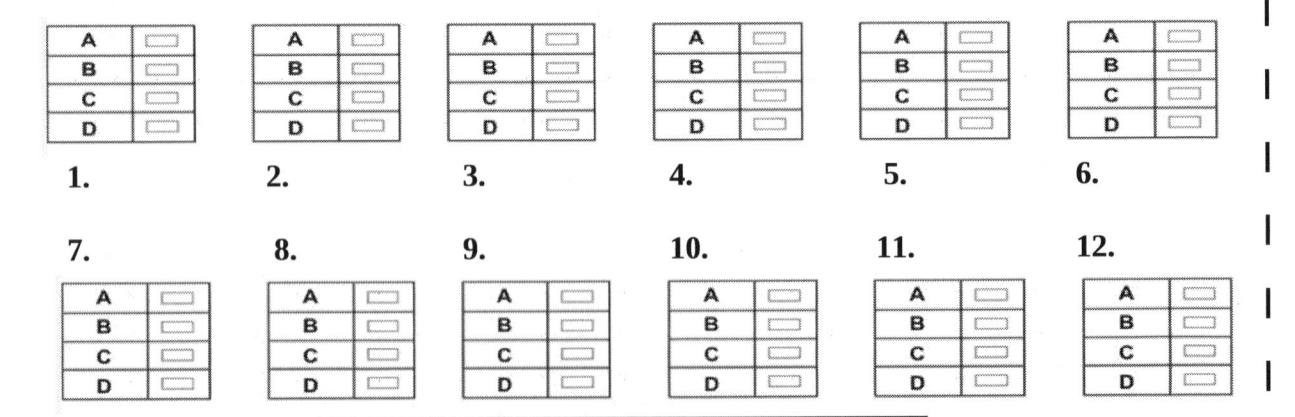

1.

A	
B	
C	
D	

2.

A	
B	
C	
D	

3.

A	
B	
C	
D	

4.

A	
B	
C	
D	

5.

A	
B	
C	
D	

6.

A	
B	
C	
D	

7.

A	
B	
C	
D	

8.

A	
B	
C	
D	

9.

A	
B	
C	
D	

10.

A	
B	
C	
D	

11.

A	
B	
C	
D	

12.

A	
B	
C	
D	

End of this section - Stop here.

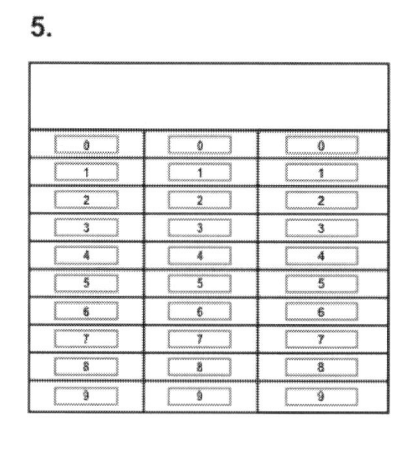

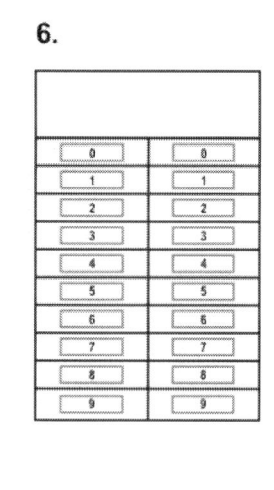

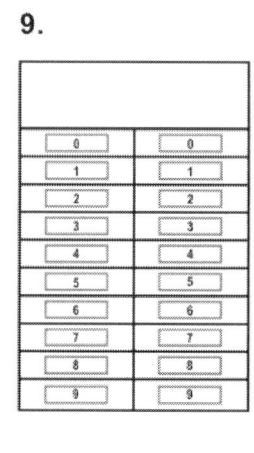

Set A Paper 1

Section 5 : Short Maths

1.
2.
3.
4.
5.
6.
7.
8.
9.
10.

Set A Paper 1

Section 5 : Short Maths (continued)

11.

12.

13. %

14. £

15. m

16.

17.

18. /

19. cm

20. £

21.

End of this section - Stop here.

Set A Paper 2

Section 1 : Numerical Reasoning

1.

8	
80	
80000	
800	

2.

0.24	
2.41	
24.1	
0.18	
0.2	

3.

		g
0	0	0
1	1	1
2	2	2
3	3	3
4	4	4
5	5	5
6	6	6
7	7	7
8	8	8
9	9	9

4.

	days
0	0
1	1
2	2
3	3
4	4
5	5
6	6
7	7
8	8
9	9

5.

,	
0	0
1	1
2	2
3	3
4	4
5	5
6	6
7	7
8	8
9	9

6a.

£	.		
0		0	0
1		1	1
2		2	2
3		3	3
4		4	4
5		5	5
6		6	6
7		7	7
8		8	8
9		9	9

6b.

0	0
1	1
2	2
3	3
4	4
5	5
6	6
7	7
8	8
9	9

7.

	p
0	0
1	1
2	2
3	3
4	4
5	5
6	6
7	7
8	8
9	9

8a.

75	
62	
100	
90	

8b.

11-15	
16-20	
21-25	
26-30	

8c.

13	
15	
17	
19	

9.

4°c	
5°c	
6°c	
7°c	

Set A Paper 2

Section 1 : Numerical Reasoning (continued)

10.

		o
0	0	0
1	1	1
2	2	2
3	3	3
4	4	4
5	5	5
6	6	6
7	7	7
8	8	8
9	9	9

11.

4	☐
5	☐
6	☐
7	☐

12a.

12 minutes	☐
22 minutes	☐
32 minutes	☐
42 minutes	☐

12b.

14:15	☐
14:27	☐
14:45	☐
15:05	☐

12c.

19:01	☐
19:11	☐
19:21	☐
19:31	☐

13.

3/5	☐
3/10	☐
4/6	☐
4/10	☐

14.

4	☐
5	☐
6	☐
7	☐

15a.

		m²
0	0	0
1	1	1
2	2	2
3	3	3
4	4	4
5	5	5
6	6	6
7	7	7
8	8	8
9	9	9

15b.

£			.		
0	0	0		0	0
1	1	1		1	1
2	2	2		2	2
3	3	3		3	3
4	4	4		4	4
5	5	5		5	5
6	6	6		6	6
7	7	7		7	7
8	8	8		8	8
9	9	9		9	9

16.

		km
0	0	0
1	1	1
2	2	2
3	3	3
4	4	4
5	5	5
6	6	6
7	7	7
8	8	8
9	9	9

Set A Paper 2

Section 1 : Numerical Reasoning (continued)

17a.

17b.

17c.

17d.

18.

08:20	
08:30	
08:40	
08:50	

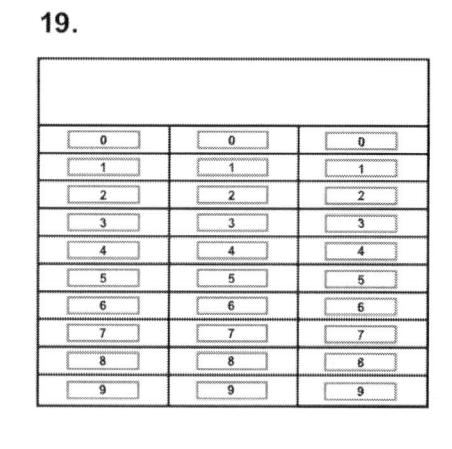

19.

20a.

20b.

Dundee	
Aberdeen	
Inverness	
Glasgow	

20c.

250	
261	
267	
273	

21.

18 litres	
20 litres	
24 litres	
26 litres	

22.

6cm	
9cm	
12cm	
18cm	

95

Set A Paper 2

Section 1 : Numerical Reasoning (continued)

23a.

6 litres	
9 litres	
12 litres	
18 litres	

23b.

| Jane | |
| Mark | |

23c.

600 litres	
900 litres	
1200 litres	
1800 litres	

24a.

0	0
1	1
2	2
3	3
4	4
5	5
6	6
7	7
8	8
9	9

24b.

2n-4	
4n-4	
4n-2	
2n+6	

25.

0	0
1	1
2	2
3	3
4	4
5	5
6	6
7	7
8	8
9	9

26.

| 0 |
| 1 |
| 2 |
| 3 |
| 4 |
| 5 |
| 6 |
| 7 |
| 8 |
| 9 |

End of this section - Stop here.

Set A Paper 2

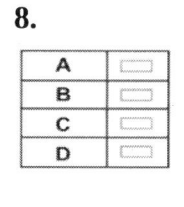

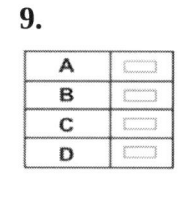

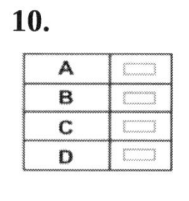

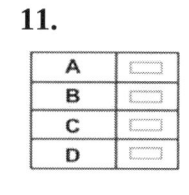

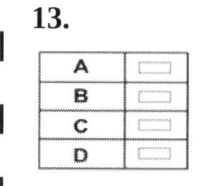

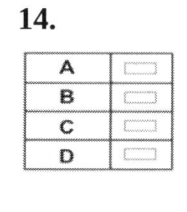

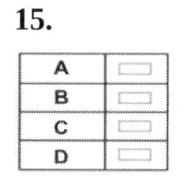

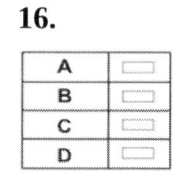

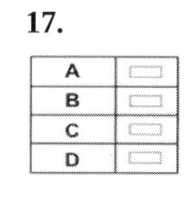

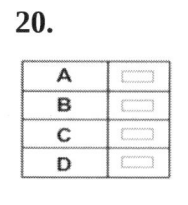

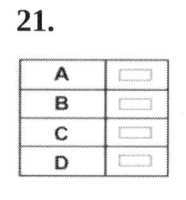

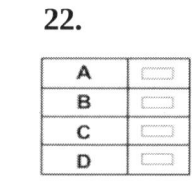

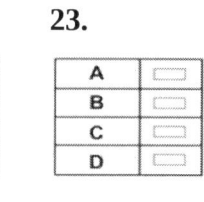

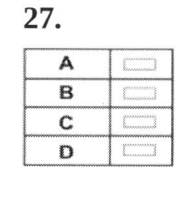

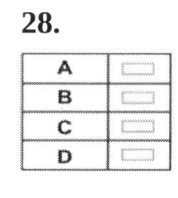

Section 2 : Non-Verbal Reasoning

1.
A	☐
B	☐
C	☐
D	☐

2.
A	☐
B	☐
C	☐
D	☐

3.
A	☐
B	☐
C	☐
D	☐

4.
A	☐
B	☐
C	☐
D	☐

5.
A	☐
B	☐
C	☐
D	☐

6.
A	☐
B	☐
C	☐
D	☐

7.
A	☐
B	☐
C	☐
D	☐

8.
A	☐
B	☐
C	☐
D	☐

9.
A	☐
B	☐
C	☐
D	☐

10.
A	☐
B	☐
C	☐
D	☐

11.
A	☐
B	☐
C	☐
D	☐

12.
A	☐
B	☐
C	☐
D	☐

13.
A	☐
B	☐
C	☐
D	☐

14.
A	☐
B	☐
C	☐
D	☐

15.
A	☐
B	☐
C	☐
D	☐

16.
A	☐
B	☐
C	☐
D	☐

17.
A	☐
B	☐
C	☐
D	☐

18.
A	☐
B	☐
C	☐
D	☐

19.
A	☐
B	☐
C	☐
D	☐

20.
A	☐
B	☐
C	☐
D	☐

21.
A	☐
B	☐
C	☐
D	☐

22.
A	☐
B	☐
C	☐
D	☐

23.
A	☐
B	☐
C	☐
D	☐

24.
A	☐
B	☐
C	☐
D	☐

25.
A	☐
B	☐
C	☐
D	☐

26.
A	☐
B	☐
C	☐
D	☐

27.
A	☐
B	☐
C	☐
D	☐

28.
A	☐
B	☐
C	☐
D	☐

29.
A	☐
B	☐
C	☐
D	☐

30.
A	☐
B	☐
C	☐
D	☐

End of this section - Stop here.

Set B Paper 1   Name:

Section 1: Comprehension

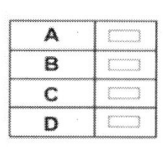

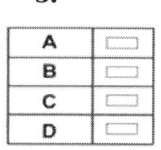

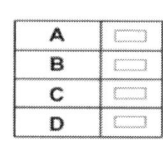

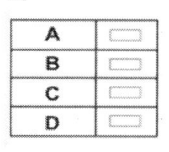

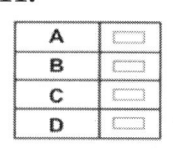

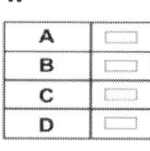

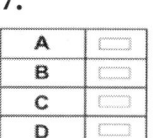

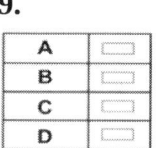

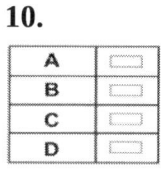

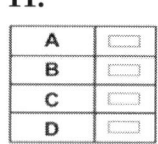

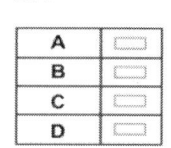

1.	2.	3.	4.	5.	6.
A ▢ B ▢ C ▢ D ▢	A ▢ B ▢ C ▢ D ▢	A ▢ B ▢ C ▢ D ▢	A ▢ B ▢ C ▢ D ▢	A ▢ B ▢ C ▢ D ▢	A ▢ B ▢ C ▢ D ▢

7.	8.	9.	10.	11.	12.
A ▢ B ▢ C ▢ D ▢	A ▢ B ▢ C ▢ D ▢	A ▢ B ▢ C ▢ D ▢	A ▢ B ▢ C ▢ D ▢	A ▢ B ▢ C ▢ D ▢	A ▢ B ▢ C ▢ D ▢

End of this section - Stop here.

Section 2: Odd one out

1.	2.	3.	4.	5.	6.
A ▢ B ▢ C ▢ D ▢	A ▢ B ▢ C ▢ D ▢	A ▢ B ▢ C ▢ D ▢	A ▢ B ▢ C ▢ D ▢	A ▢ B ▢ C ▢ D ▢	A ▢ B ▢ C ▢ D ▢

7.	8.	9.	10.	11.	12.
A ▢ B ▢ C ▢ D ▢	A ▢ B ▢ C ▢ D ▢	A ▢ B ▢ C ▢ D ▢	A ▢ B ▢ C ▢ D ▢	A ▢ B ▢ C ▢ D ▢	A ▢ B ▢ C ▢ D ▢

13.	14.	15.	16.	17.	18.
A ▢ B ▢ C ▢ D ▢	A ▢ B ▢ C ▢ D ▢	A ▢ B ▢ C ▢ D ▢	A ▢ B ▢ C ▢ D ▢	A ▢ B ▢ C ▢ D ▢	A ▢ B ▢ C ▢ D ▢

19.	20.
A ▢ B ▢ C ▢ D ▢	A ▢ B ▢ C ▢ D ▢

End of this section - Stop here.

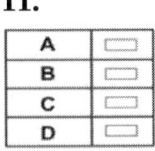

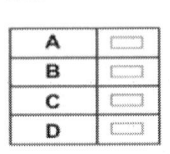

Set B Paper 1

Section 3: Antonyms

1. | A | B | C | D |
2. | A | B | C | D |
3. | A | B | C | D |
4. | A | B | C | D |
5. | A | B | C | D |
6. | A | B | C | D |
7. | A | B | C | D |
8. | A | B | C | D |
9. | A | B | C | D |
10. | A | B | C | D |
11. | A | B | C | D |
12. | A | B | C | D |
13. | A | B | C | D |
14. | A | B | C | D |
15. | A | B | C | D |
16. | A | B | C | D |
17. | A | B | C | D |
18. | A | B | C | D |
19. | A | B | C | D |
20. | A | B | C | D |

End of this section - Stop here.

Section 4 – Synonyms - missing letters

1. dusk — ☐ w ☐ l i ☐ ☐ t
2. stiff — r ☐ g ☐ d
3. inept — ☐ s e ☐ ☐ s s
4. shy — b ☐ ☐ h f u l
5. cease — t ☐ r ☐ i n ☐ ☐ e
6. buys — ☐ u r c ☐ ☐ s ☐ s
7. assist — s u ☐ p ☐ ☐ t
8. toiled — w ☐ ☐ ☐ e d
9. tedious — ☐ o ☐ ☐ n g
10. positive — ☐ p ☐ i ☐ ☐ ☐ t i c
11. occurring — ☐ a p p ☐ ☐ i ☐ g
12. revolves — r o ☐ ☐ t e s
13. embellish — ☐ ☐ c ☐ r ☐ t e
14. substantial — ☐ o n ☐ i ☐ e r ☐ ☐ e
15. dangerous — ☐ a z a r ☐ ☐ ☐ s
16. noticeable — ☐ ☐ n ☐ ☐ i c u ☐ u s
17. need — r ☐ q ☐ ☐ r e
18. adversary — o ☐ p o ☐ ☐ ☐ t

End of this section - Stop here.

Set B Paper 1

Section 5 : Short Maths

1.
2.
3.
4.
5.
6.
7.
8.
9.

Set B Paper 1

Section 5: Short Maths (continued)

10.

11.

12.

13.

14.

15.

2.473	
2.47	
2.528	
1.715	
1.7	

16.

17.

18.

19.

20.

End of this section - Stop here.

Set B Paper 2

Section 1 : Numerical Reasoning

1.

2. £

3. /

4. /

5.

6a.
BMW	
Ford	
Audi	
VW	

6b.

6c.
Jan	
Feb	
Mar	
Apr	
May	

6d.

7. /

8.

Set B Paper 2

Section 1 : Numerical Reasoning (continued)

9.

10.

11. £

12. £

13a.

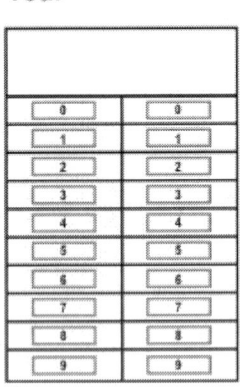

13b.

13c.

13d. %

14a.

14b.

Set B Paper 2

Section 1 : Numerical Reasoning (continued)

14c.

15a. $

15b. £

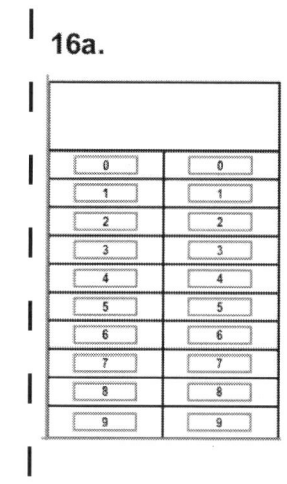

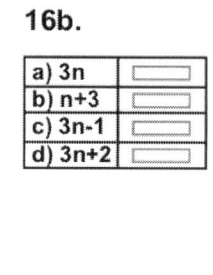

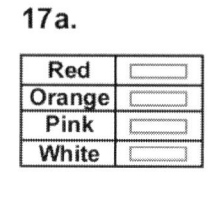

15c. £

16a.

16b.
a) 3n	
b) n+3	
c) 3n-1	
d) 3n+2	

17a.
Red	
Orange	
Pink	
White	

17b.

17c.

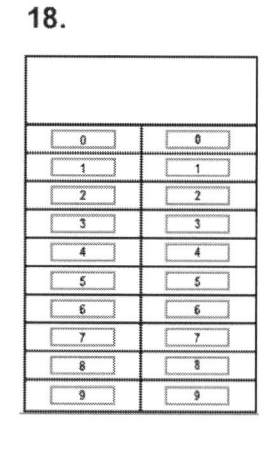

18.

19a.
(-6,0)	
(6,5)	
(0,-6)	
(0,6)	

19b.
SW	
E	
SE	
S	

Set B Paper 2

Section 1 : Numerical Reasoning (continued)

19c.

(-6,-2)	▭
(3,1)	▭
(2,2)	▭
(3,2)	▭

19d.

(-6,5)	▭
(6,-5)	▭
(6,-4)	▭
(-3,-2)	▭

20.

0	0
1	1
2	2
3	3
4	4
5	5
6	6
7	7
8	8
9	9

21.

0	0
1	1
2	2
3	3
4	4
5	5
6	6
7	7
8	8
9	9

22a.

	%
0	0
1	1
2	2
3	3
4	4
5	5
6	6
7	7
8	8
9	9

22b.

0	0
1	1
2	2
3	3
4	4
5	5
6	6
7	7
8	8
9	9

22c.

0	0
1	1
2	2
3	3
4	4
5	5
6	6
7	7
8	8
9	9

End of this section - Stop here.

Set B Paper 2

Section 2 : Non - Verbal Reasoning

1.	2.	3.	4.	5.	6.
A ☐ B ☐ C ☐ D ☐	A ☐ B ☐ C ☐ D ☐	A ☐ B ☐ C ☐ D ☐	A ☐ B ☐ C ☐ D ☐	A ☐ B ☐ C ☐ D ☐	A ☐ B ☐ C ☐ D ☐

7.	8.	9.	10.	11.	12.
A ☐ B ☐ C ☐ D ☐	A ☐ B ☐ C ☐ D ☐	A ☐ B ☐ C ☐ D ☐	A ☐ B ☐ C ☐ D ☐	A ☐ B ☐ C ☐ D ☐	A ☐ B ☐ C ☐ D ☐

13.	14.	15.	16.	17.	18.
A ☐ B ☐ C ☐ D ☐	A ☐ B ☐ C ☐ D ☐	A ☐ B ☐ C ☐ D ☐	A ☐ B ☐ C ☐ D ☐	A ☐ B ☐ C ☐ D ☐	A ☐ B ☐ C ☐ D ☐

19.	20.	21.	22.	23.	24.
A ☐ B ☐ C ☐ D ☐	A ☐ B ☐ C ☐ D ☐	A ☐ B ☐ C ☐ D ☐	A ☐ B ☐ C ☐ D ☐	A ☐ B ☐ C ☐ D ☐	A ☐ B ☐ C ☐ D ☐

25.	26.	27.	28.	29.	30.
A ☐ B ☐ C ☐ D ☐	A ☐ B ☐ C ☐ D ☐	A ☐ B ☐ C ☐ D ☐	A ☐ B ☐ C ☐ D ☐	A ☐ B ☐ C ☐ D ☐	A ☐ B ☐ C ☐ D ☐

End of this section - Stop here.

Set A Paper 1

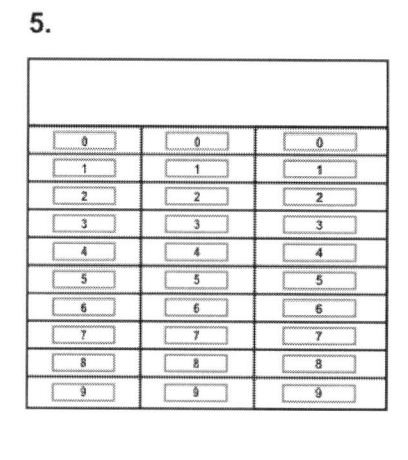

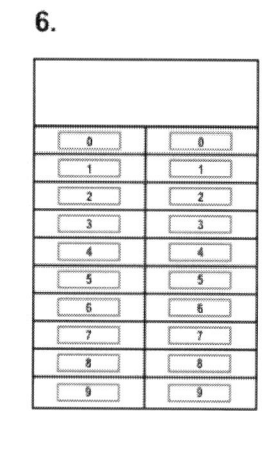

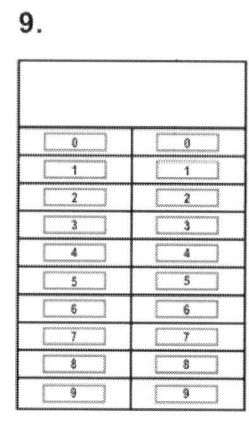

Section 5 : Short Maths

1.
2.
3.
4.
5.
6.
7.
8.
9.
10.

Set A Paper 1

Section 5 : Short Maths (continued)

11.

12.

13. %

14. £

15. m

16.

17.

18. /

19. cm

20. £

21.

End of this section - Stop here.

Set A Paper 2

Section 1 : Numerical Reasoning

1.
8	
80	
80000	
800	

2.
0.24	
2.41	
24.1	
0.18	
0.2	

3. g

4. days

5. ,

6a. £

6b.

7. p

8a.
75	
62	
100	
90	

8b.
11-15	
16-20	
21-25	
26-30	

8c.
13	
15	
17	
19	

9.
4°c	
5°c	
6°c	
7°c	

Set A Paper 2

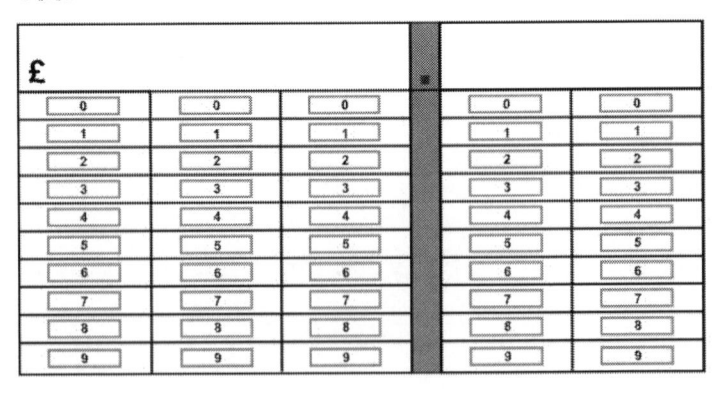

Section 1 : Numerical Reasoning (continued)

10. (answer grid, 3 digits, units: o)

11.
4	
5	
6	
7	

12a.
12 minutes	
22 minutes	
32 minutes	
42 minutes	

12b.
14:15	
14:27	
14:45	
15:05	

12c.
19:01	
19:11	
19:21	
19:31	

13.
3/5	
3/10	
4/6	
4/10	

14.
4	
5	
6	
7	

15a. (answer grid, 3 digits, units: m²)

15b. (answer grid, £, with decimal point, 3 digits and 2 digits)

16. (answer grid, 3 digits, units: km)

Set A Paper 2

Section 1 : Numerical Reasoning (continued)

17a.

17b.

17c.

17d.

18.

08:20	
08:30	
08:40	
08:50	

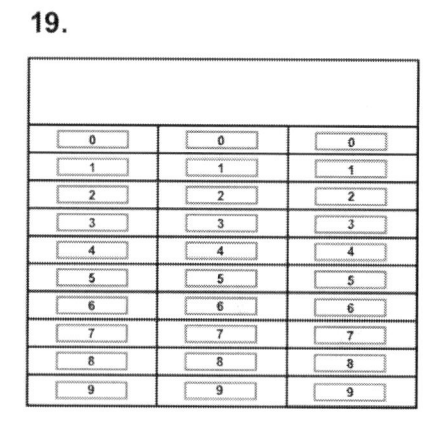

19.

20a.

20b.

Dundee	
Aberdeen	
Inverness	
Glasgow	

20c.

250	
261	
267	
273	

21.

18 litres	
20 litres	
24 litres	
26 litres	

22.

6cm	
9cm	
12cm	
18cm	

Set A Paper 2

Section 1 : Numerical Reasoning (continued)

23a.

6 litres	
9 litres	
12 litres	
18 litres	

23b.

| Jane | |
| Mark | |

23c.

600 litres	
900 litres	
1200 litres	
1800 litres	

24a.

0	0
1	1
2	2
3	3
4	4
5	5
6	6
7	7
8	8
9	9

24b.

2n-4	
4n-4	
4n-2	
2n+6	

25.

0	0
1	1
2	2
3	3
4	4
5	5
6	6
7	7
8	8
9	9

26.

| 0 |
| 1 |
| 2 |
| 3 |
| 4 |
| 5 |
| 6 |
| 7 |
| 8 |
| 9 |

End of this section - Stop here.

Set B Paper 1

Name:

Section 1: Comprehension

1.	2.	3.	4.	5.	6.
A	A	A	A	A	A
B	B	B	B	B	B
C	C	C	C	C	C
D	D	D	D	D	D

7.	8.	9.	10.	11.	12.
A	A	A	A	A	A
B	B	B	B	B	B
C	C	C	C	C	C
D	D	D	D	D	D

End of this section - Stop here.

Section 2 : Odd one out

1.	2.	3.	4.	5.	6.
A	A	A	A	A	A
B	B	B	B	B	B
C	C	C	C	C	C
D	D	D	D	D	D

7.	8.	9.	10.	11.	12.
A	A	A	A	A	A
B	B	B	B	B	B
C	C	C	C	C	C
D	D	D	D	D	D

13.	14.	15.	16.	17.	18.
A	A	A	A	A	A
B	B	B	B	B	B
C	C	C	C	C	C
D	D	D	D	D	D

19.	20.
A	A
B	B
C	C
D	D

End of this section - Stop here.

Set B Paper 1

Section 3: Antonyms

1.

A	▭
B	▭
C	▭
D	▭

2.

A	▭
B	▭
C	▭
D	▭

3.

A	▭
B	▭
C	▭
D	▭

4.

A	▭
B	▭
C	▭
D	▭

5.

A	▭
B	▭
C	▭
D	▭

6.

A	▭
B	▭
C	▭
D	▭

7.

A	▭
B	▭
C	▭
D	▭

8.

A	▭
B	▭
C	▭
D	▭

9.

A	▭
B	▭
C	▭
D	▭

10.

A	▭
B	▭
C	▭
D	▭

11.

A	▭
B	▭
C	▭
D	▭

12.

A	▭
B	▭
C	▭
D	▭

13.

A	▭
B	▭
C	▭
D	▭

14.

A	▭
B	▭
C	▭
D	▭

15.

A	▭
B	▭
C	▭
D	▭

16.

A	▭
B	▭
C	▭
D	▭

17.

A	▭
B	▭
C	▭
D	▭

18.

A	▭
B	▭
C	▭
D	▭

19.

A	▭
B	▭
C	▭
D	▭

20.

A	▭
B	▭
C	▭
D	▭

End of this section - Stop here.

Section 4 – Synonyms - missing letters

1. dusk — □ w □ l i □ □ t
2. stiff — r □ g □ d
3. inept — □ s e □ □ s s
4. shy — b □ □ h f u l
5. cease — t □ r □ i n □ □ e
6. buys — □ u r c □ □ s □ s
7. assist — s u □ p □ □ t
8. toiled — w □ □ □ e d
9. tedious — □ o □ □ n g
10. positive — □ p □ i □ □ □ t i c
11. occurring — □ a p p □ □ i □ g
12. revolves — r o □ □ t e s
13. embellish — □ □ c □ r □ t e
14. substantial — □ o n □ i □ e r □ □ □ e
15. dangerous — □ a z a r □ □ □ s
16. noticeable — □ □ n □ □ i c u □ u s
17. need — r □ q □ □ r e
18. adversary — o □ p o □ □ □ t

End of this section - Stop here.

Set B Paper 1

Section 5 : Short Maths

1.
2.
3.
4.
5.
6.
7.
8.
9.

Set B Paper 1

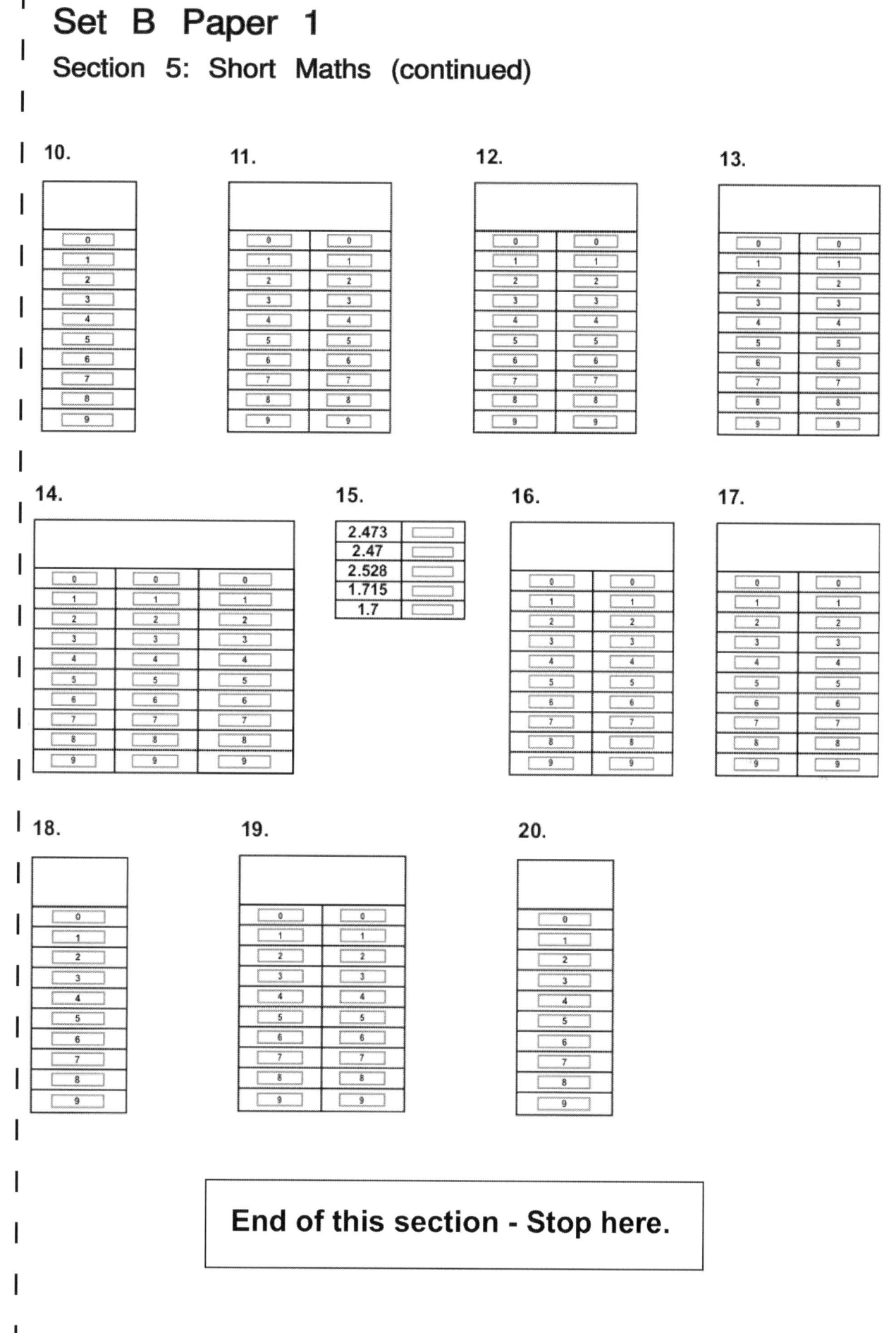

Section 5: Short Maths (continued)

10.

0
1
2
3
4
5
6
7
8
9

11.

0	0
1	1
2	2
3	3
4	4
5	5
6	6
7	7
8	8
9	9

12.

0	0
1	1
2	2
3	3
4	4
5	5
6	6
7	7
8	8
9	9

13.

0	0
1	1
2	2
3	3
4	4
5	5
6	6
7	7
8	8
9	9

14.

0	0	0
1	1	1
2	2	2
3	3	3
4	4	4
5	5	5
6	6	6
7	7	7
8	8	8
9	9	9

15.

2.473	
2.47	
2.528	
1.715	
1.7	

16.

0	0
1	1
2	2
3	3
4	4
5	5
6	6
7	7
8	8
9	9

17.

0	0
1	1
2	2
3	3
4	4
5	5
6	6
7	7
8	8
9	9

18.

0
1
2
3
4
5
6
7
8
9

19.

0	0
1	1
2	2
3	3
4	4
5	5
6	6
7	7
8	8
9	9

20.

0
1
2
3
4
5
6
7
8
9

End of this section - Stop here.

Set B Paper 2

Section 1 : Numerical Reasoning

1.
2.
3.
4.
5.
6a.

BMW	
Ford	
Audi	
VW	

6b.
6c.

Jan	
Feb	
Mar	
Apr	
May	

6d.
7.
8.

Set B Paper 2

Section 1 : Numerical Reasoning (continued)

9.

10.

11. £

12. £

13a.

13b.

13c.

13d. %

14a.

14b.

Set B Paper 2

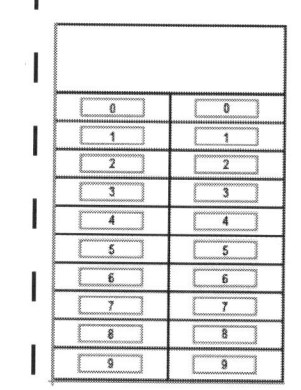

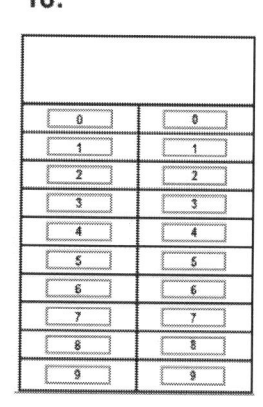

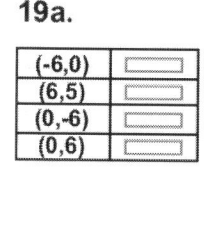

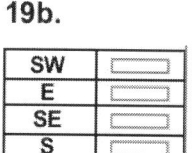

Section 1 : Numerical Reasoning (continued)

14c.

0	0
1	1
2	2
3	3
4	4
5	5
6	6
7	7
8	8
9	9

15a.

$
0
1
2
3
4
5
6
7
8
9

15b.

£
0
1
2
3
4
5
6
7
8
9

15c.

£
0
1
2
3
4
5
6
7
8
9

16a.

0	0
1	1
2	2
3	3
4	4
5	5
6	6
7	7
8	8
9	9

16b.

a) 3n	
b) n+3	
c) 3n-1	
d) 3n+2	

17a.

Red	
Orange	
Pink	
White	

17b.

0	0
1	1
2	2
3	3
4	4
5	5
6	6
7	7
8	8
9	9

17c.

0	0
1	1
2	2
3	3
4	4
5	5
6	6
7	7
8	8
9	9

18.

0	0
1	1
2	2
3	3
4	4
5	5
6	6
7	7
8	8
9	9

19a.

(-6,0)	
(6,5)	
(0,-6)	
(0,6)	

19b.

SW	
E	
SE	
S	

Set B Paper 2

Section 1 : Numerical Reasoning (continued)

19c.

(-6,-2)	
(3,1)	
(2,2)	
(3,2)	

19d.

(-6,5)	
(6,-5)	
(6,-4)	
(-3,-2)	

20.

21.

22a.

22b.

22c.

End of this section - Stop here.

Set B Paper 2

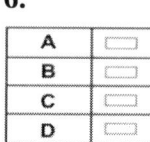

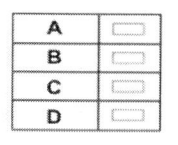

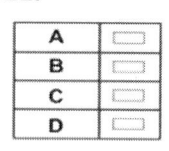

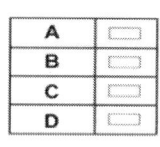

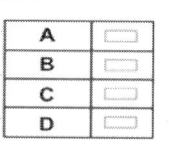

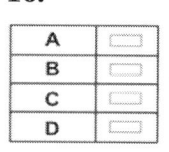

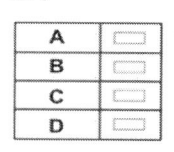

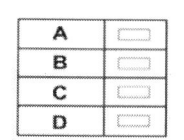

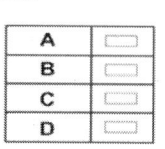

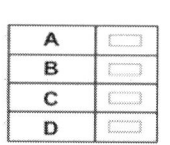

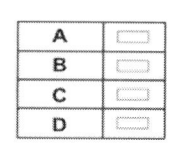

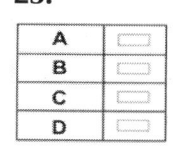

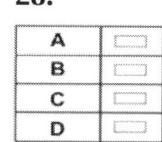

Section 2 : Non - Verbal Reasoning

1.
A	☐
B	☐
C	☐
D	☐

2.
A	☐
B	☐
C	☐
D	☐

3.
A	☐
B	☐
C	☐
D	☐

4.
A	☐
B	☐
C	☐
D	☐

5.
A	☐
B	☐
C	☐
D	☐

6.
A	☐
B	☐
C	☐
D	☐

7.
A	☐
B	☐
C	☐
D	☐

8.
A	☐
B	☐
C	☐
D	☐

9.
A	☐
B	☐
C	☐
D	☐

10.
A	☐
B	☐
C	☐
D	☐

11.
A	☐
B	☐
C	☐
D	☐

12.
A	☐
B	☐
C	☐
D	☐

13.
A	☐
B	☐
C	☐
D	☐

14.
A	☐
B	☐
C	☐
D	☐

15.
A	☐
B	☐
C	☐
D	☐

16.
A	☐
B	☐
C	☐
D	☐

17.
A	☐
B	☐
C	☐
D	☐

18.
A	☐
B	☐
C	☐
D	☐

19.
A	☐
B	☐
C	☐
D	☐

20.
A	☐
B	☐
C	☐
D	☐

21.
A	☐
B	☐
C	☐
D	☐

22.
A	☐
B	☐
C	☐
D	☐

23.
A	☐
B	☐
C	☐
D	☐

24.
A	☐
B	☐
C	☐
D	☐

25.
A	☐
B	☐
C	☐
D	☐

26.
A	☐
B	☐
C	☐
D	☐

27.
A	☐
B	☐
C	☐
D	☐

28.
A	☐
B	☐
C	☐
D	☐

29.
A	☐
B	☐
C	☐
D	☐

30.
A	☐
B	☐
C	☐
D	☐

End of this section - Stop here.

Set A Paper 1 Answers

Section 1 – Comprehension
1. c
2. c
3. b
4. a
5. d
6. a
7. b
8. c
9. d
10. b
11. d
12. c
13. a
14. d
15. a

Section 2 – Synonyms
1. b
2. c
3. a
4. d
5. d
6. a
7. b
8. d
9. b
10. a
11. d

Section 2 – Synonyms (continued)
12. b
13. c
14. a
15. b
16. d
17. a
18. b
19. d
20. c

Section 3 – CLOZE
The Lion and the bull
1. i
2. a
3. d
4. l
5. h
6. g
7. b
8. c
9. f
10. e
11. j
12. k

Section 4 – Shuffled sentences
1. c
2. a
3. b
4. c
5. d
6. a

133

Section 4 – Shuffled sentences (cont)

7. d
8. a
9. a
10. c
11. c
12. b

Section 5 – Short Maths

1. 28
2. 64
3. £13.59
4. 72
5. 225
6. 54
7. 6
8. 39
9. 30
10. 14500
11. 208
12. 25
13. 76%
14. £4.20
15. 88m
16. 15
17. 48
18. $\frac{2}{7}$
19. 7cm
20. £19.95
21. 5

Set A Paper 2 Answers

Section 1 – Numerical Reasoning
1. 80,000
2. 0.18
3. 450g
4. 12
5. (8, 9)
6a. £3.85
6b. 12
7. 70p
8a. 75
8b. 16 – 20
8c. 17
9. 7° C
10. 810°
11. 6
12a. 22 minutes
12b. 14:27
12c. 19:01
13. 4/10
14. 7
15a. 311 m²
15b. £230.79
16. 105 km
17a. 52
17b. 96
17c. 28
17d. 156
18. 08:20
19. 216

Section 1 – Numerical Reasoning (continued)
20a. 72
20b. Inverness
20c. 273
21. 26 litres
22. 9 cm
23a. 9 litres
23b. Mark
23c. 1800 litres
24a. 26
24. C) 4n – 2
25. 18
26. 5

Section 2 – Non-Verbal Reasoning
Changing shapes
1. C add a black dot to original shape and an extra swirl.
2. B add an extra loop.
3. D both shapes add an extra side. The big and small shapes swap colour.
4. A outside and inside shapes swap. The outside line becomes bold. Same number of inside shapes as lines on the outside shape.
5. D dotted lines and solid lines swap. An extra line is added to the inside lines.

Cube nets
6. D it is D because the striped lines are directly above the star and the target shape is directly to the right of the star. It is not A because the heart and star are not joining on the net. It is not B because the heart, not the star is directly above the blank side

Section 2 – Non-Verbal Reasoning
(Continued)

It is not C because the triangle would point towards the top of the heart and the blank side is to the left of the heart.

7. **C** it is C because black square is directly below curved diagonal line and the black side will fold around to be on the right of the square. Not A as all three are in a row; Not B all three in same row; Not D as curved line and straight line are two apart.

8. **A** it is A because the stripes are directly under the target and as the arrow folds around, it will point down. Not B as right-hand arrow would point up. Not C as arrow would point to the right. Not D as target and triangle are two apart.

9. **C** it is C because when the cube is turned so the black side is above the circle, the blank side is to the right. Not A as the two stars are wrong way around. Not B as large star is to right of the black and not the circle. Not D as no black star like that on the net.

10. **B** it is B because the X is to the right of the – and the ÷ would fold to be upright. Not A as + not X above the divide. Not C as = and ÷ are two apart on net. Not D as ÷ is directly to right of – and it should be X.

11. **A** it is A because the multiply is directly to the right of the tick and the horizontal stripes would fold to be above the tick. Not B as diagonal corners would be to left of horizontal lines. Not C as black side would be on left of diagonal corners. Not D as tick and vertical stripes are two apart on the net.

12. **D** it is D because if the cube was rotated, the arrow would point towards the target and be on its right while the heart would fold so the point was nearest the target. Not A as there's no white heart. Not B as the triangle should be on the left of the blank side. Not C as the target and the square are two apart on the net.

13. **D** it is D because the diagonal line is directly to the right of the crescent moon and the kite would fold round to be above the crescent moon. Not A because the striped oval and crescent are two apart on the net. Not B as the three are in a line. Not C as the pentagon cannot be on the right of the trapezium.

14. **B** it is B because the stripes are directly to the right of the rectangle and the swirl is directly above. Not A as the rectangle is black. Not C as there is no triangle on the net. Not D as all three are in a straight line.

15. **B** it is B because the diagonal stripe is to the right of the black side and the circle would fold to be on top of the black side. Not A as they are in a straight line on the net. Not C as the black side and the star are two apart on the net. Not D as the star would be to the right of the white if the stripe is above it.

Complete the series

16. **B** the shaded angle moves one place clockwise each time and an extra star is added anticlockwise.

17. **D** the number of sides increases each time and the number of dots is one less than the number of sides. The dots move 90° anticlockwise each time.

18. **C** the arrowheads alternate black and white. The number of lines increases by one each time and rotate 180°

19. **B** The cylinder alternates direction each time and the black section moves back one each time.

Section 2 – Non-Verbal Reasoning
(Continued)

20. A   the shading changes from black to white and each box has a shape with one extra line of symmetry.

Codes

21. D   A= circle   B= triangle   C= square   D= grey   E= black   F= white

22. B   A= black B= grey C= white D= up   E= down   F= right

23. A   A= clockwise B= anti-clockwise D= circle   E= square   F= triangle

24. C   A= 1 dotted line   B= 2 dotted lines C= zero dotted lines   D= 3 dotted lines   E= 3 points where lines cross F= 2 points where lines cross   G= 1 point where lines cross

25. B   A= triangle top left   B= triangle middle   C= triangle bottom right D= Black dot middle left   E= black dot top left   F= black dot bottom left

Reflect the shape

26. B   black dot must stay at top

27. A   white rectangle must stay on top

28. C   thick line must stay on top and long line must be included at bottom

29. D   one dot only at top but must face in opposite direction to original shape

30. A   bottom square must be white and small, third shape from bottom must be white.

Set B Paper 1

Answers

Section 1 – Comprehension
1. c
2. c
3. c
4. a
5. d
6. b
7. d
8. a
9. d
10. c
11. c
12. a

Section 2 – Odd one out
1. a
2. c
3. d
4. d
5. d
6. a
7. a
8. b
9. d
10. c
11. a
12. c
13. a
14. b

Section 2 – Odd one out (continued)
15. d
16. d
17. b
18. d
19. a
20. b

Section 3 – Antonyms
1. c
2. a
3. d
4. b
5. b
6. d
7. a
8. c
9. c
10. a
11. d
12. b
13. d
14. b
15. a
16. c
17. d
18. b
19. a
20. c

Section 4 – Synonyms missing letters
1. twilight
2. rigid
3. useless
4. bashful
5. terminate
6. purchases
7. support
8. worked
9. boring
10. optimistic
11. happening
12. rotates
13. decorate
14. considerable
15. hazardous
16. conspicuous
17. require
18. opponent

Section 5 – short Maths
1. 78
2. 40
3. 536
4. 53°
5. 18
6. £24.95
7. £4.05
8. 58
9. 4.6
10. 6
11. 17
12. 37
13. 10
14. 288
15. 2.528
16. 39
17. 45
18. 4
19. 41
20. 6

Set B Paper 2

Answers

Section 1 – Numerical Reasoning
1. 636
2. £4.50
3. 7/9
4. 1/3
5. 48
6a. Ford
6b. 2
6c. January
6d. 56
7. 1/4
8. 24
9. 192
10. (9,7)
11. £120
12. £47.86
13a. 10
13b. 10
13c. 13
13d. 20%
14a. 42
14b. 15
14c. 80
15a. $3
15b. £5
15c. £6
16a. 20
16b. C) 3n – 1
17a. Red
17b. 80
17c. 64
18. 42
19a. (0,-6)
19b. SE
19c. (3,1)
19d. (6,-5)
20. 14
21. 87
22a. 10%
22b. 63
22c. 84

Section 2 – Non-Verbal Reasoning
Most like the first two

1. C number of shapes inside corresponds to the number of sides on the outside shape.
2. D number of black hearts corresponds to the number of lines.
3. D number of dots is one less than the number of sides.
4. A number of shaded areas corresponds to the number of straight lines.
5. B number of dots (regardless of colour) corresponds to the number of times the lines cross.
6. B the rectangles are identical with grey trapezium in the identical place on right on base.
7. A the black shapes on the ends of the lines join to make a shape. The lines correspond to the number of lines in that shape.
8. C the two shapes have a vertical line of symmetry and identical shapes on each side

of the top and bottom but one of each shape is shaded in some way.

Section 2 – Non-Verbal Reasoning (Continued)

9. A   the shape with the fewer lines is shaded
10. D   there is a black and white dot on each end of the lines.

Cube nets

11. B   it is B because the blank side is directly above the curvy line and the side with diagonal corners would just fold down so line is in the top right corner. Not A as sides with diagonal corners will never meet. Not C as the blank side is to the left not the right of the side with diagonal corners. Not D as the triangle is black not white.

12. C   it is C because if the rectangle is upright, the ¾ Circle will be above it and the triangle to the right with the point nearest the circle. Not A as the right angle would fold to be upright. Not B as the kite is black not white. Not D as the isosceles triangle point should be towards the ¾ circle not facing away from it.

13. A   It is A because the circle shape is directly above the large star and the four point star would fold to be on the right. Not B as the black side is on the right not left of the blank side. Not C as the circle and line star are two apart and can never meet Not D as the three are in a row.

14. C   it is C because the X is directly above the = and the divide sign would be vertical when folded down. Not A as the = and circle are two apart and can never meet. Not B as the = should be directly to the right of the subtract not the divide. Not D as the divide is to the right of the x not to the left.

15. C   it is C because the black square is directly to the right of the horizontal striped line and the curvy line would fold to be vertical. Not A as the vertical stripe should be directly above the horizontal curvy line. Not B as the horizontal stripe is to the left not the right of the black square. Not D as the curvy line would fold to start at the top left.

Rotations

16. B   Not A as straight lines in middle. Not C as middle curves wrong way up. Not d as completely different shape.
17. A   Not B as flag colours around the wrong way. Not C as no circle in the middle. Not D as no circle and flag colours around the wrong way.
18. D   Not A as top circle and square are white. Not B as bottom rectangle facing wrong way. Not C as circle and rectangle are black.
19. C   Not A as top curve should be facing up. Not B as bottom curve with dot too long. Not D as top curve facing the wrong way.
20. B   not A as large dot on wrong side. Not C as 4 lines. Not D as black and stripes have swapped.

Cube plans

21. B   It is b because you can distinctly see the diagonal steps at the front of the shape but there is no shape in the back corner. Not A as no shape in corner. Not C as definitely three lines of shapes. Not D as no gap in middle of top row.

22. C   it is c because you can definitely see the columns go 2,1,2,1. Not A as it's missing the single cube in column 2. Not B as there is not a row of three in the middle. Not D as the first column has two cubes not one.

Section 2 – Non-Verbal Reasoning
(Continued)

23. D it is D because you can definitely see the gap in the row below the top. Not A as the top row only has one cube not two. Not B and the left column doesn't have three cubes in it. Not C as top row doesn't have two joined cubes.

24. C it is C because the rows step down diagonally from 3,2,1. not A because not 3 cubes in middle row. Not B as not enough cubes. Not D as there is definitely a cube in the top corner.

25. B it is b because it has an L shape left top corner and a single cube on each end. Not A as right column has one cube only. Not C as it is not even on both sides. Not D as it has 3 cubes in second column.

Odd one out

26. C all shapes have a right angle except C.

27. A all shapes have the number of little shapes inside corresponding to the number of side on the outside shape except A. The little shapes also have one more side than the outside shapes.

28. B number of arrows correspond with the number of white dots except B.

29. B All have straight zigzag lines except B.

30. A the number of lines correspond with the number of points on the stars except in A

Record your child's scores here

Set A paper 1

	Total Questions	1st attempt	2nd attempt
1. Comprehension	15		
2. Synonyms	20		
3. CLOZE	12		
4. Shuffled sentences	12		
5. Short Maths	21		
TOTAL	80		
% scored			

Set A Paper 2

	Total Questions	1st attempt	2nd attempt
1. Numerical reasoning	40		
2. Non-verbal reasoning	30		
TOTAL	70		
% scored			

Set A

	Total Questions	1st attempt	2nd attempt
Overall TOTAL	150		
Overall total % scored			

Set B paper 1

	Total Questions	1st attempt	2nd attempt
1. Comprehension	12		
2. Odd one out	20		
3. Antonyms	20		
4. Synonyms – missing letters	18		
5. Short Maths	20		
TOTAL	90		
% scored			

Set B Paper 2

	Total Questions	1st attempt	2nd attempt
1. Numerical reasoning	40		
2. Non-verbal reasoning	30		
TOTAL	70		
% scored			

Set B

	Total Questions	1st attempt	2nd attempt
Overall TOTAL	160		
Overall total % scored			

Printed in Great Britain
by Amazon